ROMAN LITERATURE

IN RELATION TO

ROMAN ART

ROMAN LITERATURE

IN RELATION TO

ROMAN ART

BY THE

REV. ROBERT BURN, M.A., LL.D. GLAS.

WITH ILLUSTRATIONS.

KENNIKAT PRESS
Port Washington, N. Y./London

ROMAN LITERATURE IN RELATION TO ROMAN ART

First published in 1888
Reissued in 1969 by Kennikat Press
Library of Congress Catalog Card No: 70-101034
SBN 8046-0701-X

Manufactured by Taylor Publishing Company   Dallas, Texas

KENNIKAT CLASSICS SERIES

PREFACE.

THESE essays are an attempt to show the cognate character of Roman Literature and Roman Art by pointing out the National tendencies of the Romans from which they both sprang. I hope that in these short studies a new interest will be given to the study of Roman History which may be carried on further by some abler hand than mine. They have been a solace and occupation to me in many hours of sickness and enforced leisure.

The vast extent of the ancient Roman Empire has naturally led me to compare it to the modern British Empire; the same mistakes have been made and are being made by the two nations both in Literature and Art. Instances of this will doubtless occur to every thoughtful man.

The illustrations are reproduced from photographs by Messrs. Walker and Boutall, and may therefore be relied upon for general correctness.

The fifth Essay is reprinted, with slight alterations and new illustrations, from my larger work, *Rome and the Campagna*, by the kind permission of Messrs. G. Bell & Sons.

R. B.

CAMBRIDGE, 1888.

CONTENTS.

		PAGE
INTRODUCTION	. . . .	I

ESSAY I.

| ROMAN PORTRAIT SCULPTURE | . . . . | 31 |

ESSAY II.

| NATIONAL AND HISTORICAL TENDENCY | . . . . | 68 |

ESSAY III.

| COMPOSITE AND COLOSSAL ART | . . . . | 102 |

ESSAY IV.

| TECHNICAL FINISH AND LUXURIOUS REFINEMENT | . . . . . | 139 |

ESSAY V.

| ROMANO-GREEK ARCHITECTURE | . . . . | 183 |

LIST OF ILLUSTRATIONS.

	PAGE
PARTHENON FRIEZE	4
FARNESE HERCULES	5
BATTLE OF AMAZONS	12
CONSULAR TRIUMPH	14
ROMAN CANEPHORUS	16
ERECTHEION	17
RELIEF ON ANTONINE PILLAR	24
MARCUS AGRIPPA	32
CLAUDIUS	33
ÆSCHINES	37
ANTONIA	43
CARACALLA	46
NERO	47
DOMITIAN	50
AUGUSTUS	52
AGRIPPINA	54
ROMAN LADY	55
VESPASIAN	57
NERVA	59
CALIGULA	61
SEVERUS	65
WOLF AND TWINS	69
TRIUMPH OF TIBERIUS	76
SCENE IN FORUM	78
FAMILY OF CÆSARS	83
NILE	87

PAGE

ANTONINE APOTHEOSIS 89

JUDGMENT OF EMPEROR 94

BURNING OF ACCOUNT BOOKS 98

TOMB OF SCIPIO 103

TOMB AT ATHENS 104

ARCH OF SEPTIMIUS SEVERUS 107

COLISEUM 111

TEMPLE OF NIKE 113

PORTA NIGRA, AT TREVES 115

CROWD ON SARCOPHAGUS 124

AMPHITHEATRE AT VERONA 134

TEPULAN AND CLAUDIAN AQUEDUCTS 135

ANTINOUS 140

HERCULES (BRONZE) 144

POMONA 147

THE WRESTLERS 151

A DANCING GIRL 153

POETUS AND ARRIA 160

VENUS CAPITOLINA 164

VENUS GENETRIX 166

APOLLO BENDING BOW 171

VENUS ANADYOMENE 175

CLOACA MAXIMA 192

TEMPLE AT GIRGENTI 199

TEMPLE OF SATURN 205

CAPITALS OF COLUMNS 209

ARCH OF CONSTANTINE 224

BASILICA OF CONSTANTINE 240

PORTA FURBA 268

JANUS QUADRIFRONS 279

ROMAN LITERATURE

IN RELATION TO

ROMAN ART

ROMAN LITERATURE AND ART.

INTRODUCTION.

To trace some of the erroneous tendencies of Roman literary and glyptic art, and to shew how they had their origin in the national character and circumstances of the Romans, is the endeavour of these essays. The prevalent emotions and the ideas of a nation are expressed in its literature and in its art, and these emotions and ideas are some of them peculiar to the national character, while some are produced by the national circumstances. I shall endeavour to shew the original bent of the Roman character, and its modifications as affected by circumstances. But in order to criticize the faults into which Roman art was liable to fall we had better begin by tracing the ideal to which they aspired, and then shew how these aspirations were checked or modified,

B

A passage from Cicero's writings is quoted hereafter, which shews that he valued a mental ideal as the highest point to which art could reach. The Romans as well as the Greeks ascribed it to a divine inspiration. Horace distinctly says that the Greeks derived their powers of poetic art from the Muses,

> Graiis ingenium, Graiis dedit ore rotundo
> Musa loqui.—*Ars Poet.* 323.

And we have an acknowledgment from him that the arts were introduced into Latium by the Greeks :

> Graecia capta ferum victorem cepit, et artes
> Intulit agresti Latio.—*Ep.* ii. 1, 156.

Now what the Romans thought they themselves received from the gods and what they valued most was imperial power :

> Tu regere imperio populos, Romane, memento ;
> Hae tibi erunt artes ; pacisque imponere morem,
> Parcere subiectis, et debellare superbos.—*Æn.* vi. 852.

The ideal in matters of taste was only derived by them from the gods through the medium of another nation. Their own notion of the highest of all things, their *summum bonum*, was not the beautiful, but the powerful. And this they thought they had as a nation received from heaven.

Let us take, first, imperial influences among the Romans. Roman poetic art attained its culminating point under Virgil, and it may be said that Roman sculpture rose to its grandest elevation under the Emperors Titus and Trajan. In Ovid's adherence to strict rule and in the vagueness of Statius we see the incipient stages of imperial influence, which finally ruined Latin poetry, and in the sculpture of their busts and the arch of Severus we see the same influence degrading sculpture. To trace those influences in poetry among writers subsequent to Augustus, and in sculpture among artists subsequent to Trajan is the purpose of this attempt. Such an attempt is perhaps rash and impossible, but it lends an interest to classical literature and art which cannot be surpassed, and if it should be seen that English literature and art are passing through the same stages and are subject to the same influences as was Roman, it cannot be denied that a wish to state and to check or to modify the effect of such tendencies ought to be encouraged.

It may be seen in most sculpture galleries, by comparing the Farnese Hercules (see p. 5) with the sculptured figures of the Parthenon, how the influence of imperial admiration for finish and detailed symmetry before grandeur and large idealism ruined Roman taste ; or, by comparing the busts of Brutus, Marius, or Seneca and Corbulo, with the heads

of the statues of Sophocles and Demosthenes, which last
are of Greek origin, what was the strength of the imitative
and historical tone of sculpture at Rome, or by comparing

PARTHENON FRIEZE.

the Medici Venus with the Venus of Melos, what was the
sensual feeling encouraged by wealth in a great imperial
nation; or, by comparing the Laocoon with the fighting

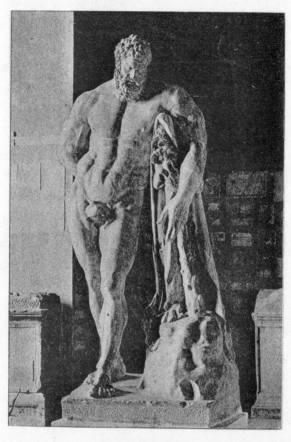

FARNESE HERCULES.

Greeks and Centaurs in Greek metopes, how technical finish alone was encouraged by patronage, while beauty of ideal motive underlying was neglected. By comparing the statue of Augustus from *prima porta* with those of Harmodius and Aristogeiton, we shall see how realism was encouraged; by comparing the Roman carved caryatid figures (see p. 16) with the straightness of the Greek ones, how the Roman threw away the strictly architectural character of the sculptures, and yielded to his fondness for sensual gratification.

It is often hastily concluded that Roman literature and Roman art are not worth our attention. The Romans, it is said, were evidently a nation devoid of the spiritual grace and noble power wherewith the Greeks earned the admiration of the world, by having produced everlasting types of beauty in poetry and in art. And it must be acknowledged that, from a strictly accurate artistic point of view, this is in a great measure true. But to those who inquire not only into the productive character of the people whose life they wish to understand, but also into the effects which national character and external circumstances had in altering and moulding their productions, a study of Roman literature and art as the results of Roman character and Roman circumstances is very valuable. They can thus ascertain the modes in which human nature is affected in similar cases, and can give warnings, or make predictions, or shew what is hazardous in national art.

The more lofty spirits among the Romans no doubt

lifted themselves above the atmosphere in which they were compelled to live, because they had studied the great writers of Greek philosophy and poetry. Hence, Cicero says, as before mentioned, that more beautiful images can be conceived in the mind than seen by the eye:

Sed ego sic statuo nihil esse in ullo genere tam pulchrum quo non pulchrius id sit unde illud ut ex ore aliquo quasi imago, exprimatur quod neque oculis neque auribus neque ullo sensu percipi potest cogitatione tantum et mente complectimur.—*Orat.* ii. 8.

And he goes on in a passage which is often quoted to say that even more beautiful statues or pictures than the best which we know can be imagined in the mind. We must therefore except such men as Cicero from our general criticism of the Romans.

Nor must we deny lofty aspirations to Roman poets. Horace in his *Ars Poetica* strikes this principal chord at once when he calls on the poet to avoid selfish pride in his own powers and to aim higher:

Nec sic incipies ut scriptor cyclicus olim:
" Fortunam Priami cantabo..."
Quanto rectius hic, qui nil molitur inepte !
" Dic mihi, Musa, virum,..." &c., &c.—*Ars Poet.* 136.

This was always done by the artists who raised Greek art to its highest level. They began with an appeal to

their gods, and by their brilliant powers of generalisation
and idealisation soared above into a supernatural region.
We have elsewhere remarked that the *Iliad* begins, as
Horace advises, with a prayer to the Muse, while the *Æneid*
breaks this rule and throws all the weight on the poet's
shoulders, as if he were competent to bear it, and could
ascend into a spiritual atmosphere without looking beyond
himself.   Spiritual thought as one of the highest attributes
of man is mentioned in one of Sophocles' most beautiful
choruses—

ἐδιδάξατο ἀνεμόεν φρόνημα ἄνθρωπος.—*Antig.* 353.

And in the majestic odes of Æschylus we have the
same superhuman feeling as in the Zeus of Phidias, which
inspired awe, and did not profess to do more than to lead
the minds of men in an ascent towards the unattainable in
might and grandeur.

Who can read some of the lines of Æschylus in the
Agamemnon—

Ζῆνα δέ τις προφρόνως ἐπινίκια κλάζων
τεύξεται φρενῶν τὸ πᾶν·
τὸν φρονεῖν βροτοὺς ὁδώσαντα τὸν πάθει μάθος
θέντα κυρίως ἔχειν.—*Ag.* 172.

without feeling how the poet is humbling himself
before one who is far above and superior to the children
of men ?

This lofty aim of poetry and art among the Greeks was not pursued far by the Romans, who contented themselves with a practical and realistic view of fine art and made their Emperor the highest ideal to which they rose. Hence Roman sculpture to a great extent employed itself in deifying men. The influence of the Christian faith at a later time gradually raised this old grovelling Roman materialism; but sculpture among the Romans never soared high, and painting took the place of sculpture in spiritualising art. Thus there has been no great Christian sculptor to compare with the great Christian painters, and the chief development of the Christian influence on art, besides painting, has been in the great cathedral architecture which has elevated and enlarged human thought in so many of the great cities of Europe. The characteristic tone of materialism which we see pervading all ancient Roman work, is diametrically opposed to this spiritual and upward tendency expressed by Gothic architecture, and we are therefore prepared to find Roman art and poetry deadening the elevated tone of Christianity for many centuries (see pp. 12 and 14).

We cannot therefore look with much hope to the study of Roman literature and art as lifting us into the highest regions of the beautiful in poetry or in architecture or sculpture. But it may be possible, by taking a different point of view, to shew that there are some advantages in gaining a historical and wide survey of the subject.

Some practical purposes are not recognized enough in the study of literary and artistic history. How frequently do we hear it asked, of what use the study of Greek and Latin history and language can be to those who are intended for the practical business of life. Yet it cannot be denied that the study of antiquity moulds and enlightens the human intellect in a manner which sometimes guards it from making serious and deadly blunders. And we are thus able to give to the unbelievers in the study of antiquity a reply which they are not able to dispute. In the case immediately before us it will be at once allowed that the British nation has a practical and undeniable interest. When we once see that the circumstances under which Englishmen are now led to carry out great works both in literature and in art resemble those which developed and modified Roman energy, then we cannot help feeling a great interest and value in the study of this branch of Roman history.

The leading trait of Roman life was austerity, which they named *severitas*. This is, it is true, only partially present in the British character and in a modified manner. In Rome it gave birth to an original form in literature, namely, Satire, veins of which run through most of the earlier

Roman poetical productions, and shew themselves widely in Roman portrait sculpture. Every one will recognize the same national feature in the school of English satirical poetry. An allied development, that of caricature, though it does not occupy so large a space as did satire among the Romans, appears very distinctly in British national art. Another Roman characteristic, which gives a tone to Roman poetry and art is also prominent in English art namely, extreme realism or materialism, or, as it is colloquially termed, a tendency to matter of fact. Both nations Roman and British have shewn in their poetry and art an admiration for the strictly historical rather than the legendary and mythical, and have combined these two features of art in a mode seldom found elsewhere. The mythical predominates over the historical far more in Greek than in Roman art. Compare for instance the Æginetan or the Gjolbaschi groups with those in the triumphal arch reliefs. From this realism also resulted in some measure that admiration for technical skill and finish which crippled Roman, and endangers British art.

But when we consider the external circumstances which modified Roman, as they are still modifying English literature and art, more striking resemblances between the consequent national productions will be at once discerned. A vast empire has been expanded by the heroic determina-

BATTLE OF AMAZONS.

tion of the British nation and by their liberal readiness to share and improve rather than to rule despotically over those portions of the earth in which they have made themselves superior to all others. But a similarly wide imperial power produced an overbearing national conceit in the Romans. It has been happily modified in the English nation to a national pride, but its effects have been felt in the conglomerate and confused features of English, as they were in those of Roman art, and it is in this direction that the simplicity of the Greek models is so correctively useful. And we must not forget the other natural consequence of imperial sway, the wealth which it places in the hands of powerful men.

This produces admiration of technical skill, colossal production, and expensive outlay, which had a powerful influence on Roman, as it also has had on British art. We can make these three—national pride, confused conglomeration, and technical degradation, our compartments in which to arrange the effects of empire upon the Romans. No reader of Pliny or of the Roman satirists will be ignorant of their severe remarks upon all these tendencies ; and few of the present generation of Britons can forget the criticism and caricature which have been launched at the coarse exaggeration of the Iron Duke, or the golden memorial of the Prince Consort. An iron statue of Hercules was made,

it is true, under the successors of Alexander by Alcon, a Rhodian artist of no eminence, and shews a somewhat similar degradation of Greek art. But we must remember that iron was not then what it is now, just as it has been remarked that ivory and gold were not the same. This is mentioned by Pliny together with the colossal statues which abounded at Rhodes.

Place the above-mentioned Iron Duke, or the Farnese Hercules, and the ill-balanced Antonine apotheosis, by the side of statuary conceived in the true Greek spirit, such as the statues of Harmodius and Aristogeiton, the Hercules epitrapezios of Lysippus, the Belvedere torso, or the memorial of Lysimachus, and the vulgar effects of imperial sway on art will be at once recognized.

Other influences arising from wealth and imperial power, besides what we have called realism, conglomeration, and confusion, prevailed at Rome, as they do also in England. Patronage was one of the most powerful. We can trace this influence more distinctly in Roman poetry than in Roman plastic or pictorial art. Every Latin scholar will see at once that the dramatic poetry of the Romans is essentially matter of fact, as is their portrait sculpture and their architecture. So the Epic and Lyric poets, Horace and Virgil, have allowed their work to be largely coloured by a wish to please great men. This can of course be

ROMAN CANEPHORUS.

traced throughout their productions and need not be
further insisted upon.   In poetry Lucretius and Catullus
are no doubt free from the taint, but Statius, Tibullus, and
Ovid, and in sculpture the authors of the Laocoon, the

ERECTHEION.

Farnese Hercules and of the Apollos, suffer under it very
severely.   How does this influence affect them?   One
would suppose that it shewed itself in the idealisation of
their patrons' good qualities and the omission of defects.

C

But this is not the way in which the Roman mirror reflects. It is rather by representing defects or ugly facts or deformities as beauties. And this appears equally in their art as in their poetry. In fact the most permeating and refracting component of the Roman character to which we shall most frequently have to ascribe changes and modifications in the types which they adopted was the above - mentioned determined materialistic or realistic tendency of their nature. The peculiarity of this tendency in the Romans was that they imitated deformity as well as beauty.

Every student of the history of art will at once recall many instances of this tendency in modern as well as in ancient times. Italian schools of art have vibrated between the two extremes of the 'bello ideale' and the 'brutto reale,' as we learn from the autobiographies of Cellini, Alfieri, d'Azeglio, and from the lately-published *Thoughts on Art* by Giovanni Dupré. In England the names of Hogarth and the school of the pre-Raphaelites will at once occur to every one.

Now one point of view from which I should wish to survey the productions of art which the Romans left to us may be shewn by taking an illustration from natural science. In trying to account for the peculiar features of rock and mountain scenery, we have not only to consider

the external effects of climate or position, but also the
internal forces by which different masses of material are
grouped and shaped. Thus in one of the most familiar
ranges of mountain outline, that of the Alpine summits,
varieties of shape are not produced more by exposure to
climatic influences than by internal mineralogical consti-
tuents. An experienced geologist could decide at once by
a glance at the outline of a peak or subordinate rock to
what kind of rock or class of formation it belongs. And
in like manner typical forms can be traced in the artistic
productions of nations, by which the historical student can
at once infer their true classification, and can delineate the
special national characteristics or external circumstances
from which they have been evolved. Perhaps another
illustration also taken from nature may make my meaning
more clear. Every one has probably noticed in marshy
districts, especially if he has travelled in the Eastern
deserts or on Oriental rivers, the great distortions and
contractions or enlargements caused by what is called
mirage. Now I wish to shew in what ways the mirage
of the Roman character and circumstances affected the
work of their poets and artists, when they tried to copy
their ideal. To take a third example in which the same
kind of refraction occurs. When we study Pope's translation of Homer, or in fact any translation into modern

verse of an ancient Greek or Latin poet, we can at once
trace the effect of the modern mind in altering language,
simile and construction, and we can discern the special
effects of the translator's surroundings.

I wish then to point out some formations and classes
in Roman literature and art produced under the special
influences of Roman national life. Let us begin with
traits of national character and then pass on to external
circumstances. As we mentioned above, one distinguish-
ing feature of the Roman mind is said to have been its
severitas or austerity. This quality shews itself throughout
Roman history. Every one will be able to call to mind
austere Roman heroes whose branding judgments on
their fellow-countrymen were so strict and severe in the
early times of Rome. But let us descend at once to the
great period of Roman development, the Augustan period.
When Horace says that examples must be drawn from
life,

> Respicere exemplar vitae morumque jubebo
> Doctum imitatorem, et veras hinc ducere voces.[1]
>
> *Ars Poet.* 317,

he is only urging what he himself saw to be one of the
natural bents of Roman *severitas*. He employs Stoic

---

[1] I bid the man who is learning to imitate to look at some model
of life or character, and to draw life for his words from that.

criticism which paints the extravagances of human life. And we can trace this feature throughout his Epistles and Satires. Quintilian says of Horace that he is acute in discerning character,

ad notandos hominum mores praecipuus —*Inst. Or.* x. 1. 94.

But cynicism in Horace is even and humorously calm. His musical bore Tigellius, and his glutton Catius are touched with light and easy wit, while Juvenal would have passed by the musical pedant as not worth notice, and we know the colours in which he has painted the glutton. Horace's Tiresias, in his amusing advice to Ulysses, draws the character of the Roman fortune-hunter in strong outlines,

Leniter in spem
Adrepe officiosus.—*Sat.* ii. 5, 47.

'Gently proceed in hope' is the tone of his precepts, and he is finally content when he hears the award, 'Let Ulysses have a fourth part',

Quartae esto partis Ulysses.—*Id.* 100.

Other model figures in Horace are drawn under his characters of Ofellus, the old-fashioned Roman farmer who entertains his friends,

Non piscibus urbe petitis,
Sed pullo atque haedo.—*Sat.* ii. 2, 121.

and of Stertinius, who sums up his philosophy in a line,

> Danda est hellebori multo pars maxima avaris.
>
> *Sat.* ii. 3, 82.

recommending the cures used for madness.

Other social influences shew themselves in the great writers of the imperial times. They felt distinctly what the great social dangers were from which Roman art, both literary and plastic, could not withdraw itself—the temptations to multifarious enunciations and to grandiose excess by which it was surrounded. Some of them gave way to these, others resisted. The Roman empire was in the Augustan days expanding and growing at an intoxicating pace, and the crowd and hurry of the metropolis were destroying simplicity of thought and life. Hence we have many passages in Horace :

> At simul atras
> Ventum est Esquilias, aliena negotia centum
> Per caput et circa saliunt latus.   Ante secundam
> Roscius orabat, sibi adesses ad Puteal cras
> De re communi scribae magna atque nova te
> Orabant hodie meminisses, Quinte, reverti.
>
> *Sat.* ii. 6, 32.

In Rome it was always a struggle,

> Luctandum in turba et facienda iniuria tardis.
>
> *Sat.* ii. 6, 28.

and abroad the 'strenua inertia' was pushing people from place to place till they could not rest.

> Navibus atque
> Quadrigis petimus bene vivere.
> *Ep.* i. 11, 29.

The effects of imperial magnificence on the spirit of the Augustan age were foreseen by Horace when he wrote his cautions—

> Professus grandia turget.—*Ars Poet.* 27.
> Sedulitas autem stulte, quem diligit, urget
> Praecipue cum se numeris commendat et arte :
> Discit enim citius meminitque libentius illud
> Quod quis deridet, quam quod probat et veneratur.
> *Ep.* ii. 1, 260-

against turgidity and strict exactitude in judgment.

National and military and imperial pride also exercised of course a strong influence at Rome. Although Horace was well aware of the perils to which art was exposed by the world-wide dominion of Rome, yet he could not in his *Odes* refrain from encouraging the national pride of empire :

> Quicunque mundo terminus obstitit,
> Hunc tangat armis.—*Od.* iii. 3, 53.

Virgil went still further, and was not ashamed to avow an almost menial worship of imperial power in his famous lines,

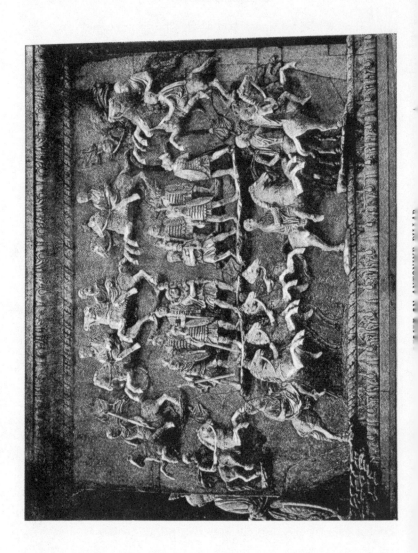

PLATE III. THE SIEGE OF ROME

Excudent alii spirantia mollius aera,
Credo equidem, vivos ducent de marmore voltus,
Orabunt causas melius, caelique meatus
Describent radio et surgentia sidera dicent :
Tu regere imperio populos, Romane, memento ;
Hae tibi erunt artes.—*Æn.* vi. 848.

Roman national glory is of course the main subject of the
Æneid. The nation wearing the toga are the masters of
the world, and the house of Æneas is destined by the
oracle to rule in all lands. The liberal and cosmopolitan
feelings produced by world-wide sway are not reconciled
or advised by Virgil, and the memory of national heroes
has with him only one object, that of inspiriting the
militant power of their descendants and thus exalting
Rome above all the world. Unbroken secular ascendency
is the fate to which the prophetic genius of the Æneid
looks forward,

Jure omnia bella
Gente sub Assaraci fato ventura resident.

Æn. ix. 642.

This is the final utterance of Apollo.

The deification of imperial personages is, of course, a
main feature in the Latin poets of the Augustan and
succeeding epochs. The invisible world of faith was united
by Virgil and Horace with the human figure and political
powers of Augustus. This has been admirably drawn out

by Otto Jahn in his comparison of the *Carmen Saeculare* of Horace with the famous statue of Augustus found at Prima Porta and now in the Braccio Nuovo of the Vatican. The adjurations of deities in this song—of Phoebus and Diana, Sol, Ilithyia, and the Parcae—are all associated with the Emperor Augustus, a scion of the great clan of Anchises and the blood of Venus, before whose potent sway the Mede, the proud Scythian and the Indian are trembling. In the third and fourth books of the *Odes* again we have many stanzas connecting the gods and the imperial dynasty :

> Hac arte Pollux et vagus Hercules
> Enisus arces attigit igneas :
>   Quos inter Augustus recumbens
>   Purpureo bibit ore nectar.—*Od.* iii. 3, 9.
> Caelo Tonantem credidimus Jovem
> Regnare : praesens divus habebitur
>   Augustus adjectis Britannis
>   Imperio gravibusque Persis.—*Od.* iii. 5, 1.
> Te copias, te consilium et tuos
> Praebente divos.—*Od.* iv. 14, 33.
> Lucem redde tuae, dux bone, patriae.—*Od.* iv. 5, 5.
> Praesenti tibi maturos largimur honores.
>   *Ep.* ii. 1, 15.

In Virgil the divine powers of Augustus are invoked to aid the Italian farmers no less than the Roman armies. Thus we have the invocations in the first *Georgic*,

Ignarosque viae mecum miseratus agrestes
Ingredere, et votis iam nunc adsuesce vocari.

Georg. I, 41.

And the celebrated outburst of worship put into the mouth
of Anchises in the sixth book of the *Æneid:*

Hic vir, hic est, tibi quem promitti saepius audis,
Augustus Caesar, Divi genus, aurea condet
Saecula qui rursus Latio regnata per arva
Saturno quondam.— *Æen.* vi. 792.

And again in the eighth book the figure of Cæsar is
represented on the shield of Æneas:

Hinc Augustus agens Italos in proelia Caesar
Cum Patribus Populoque, Penatibus et magnis Dis,
Stans celsa in puppi ; geminas cui tempora flammas
Laeta vomunt, patriumque aperitur vertice sidus.

Æn. viii. 678.

The *Julium sidus* is the symbol of apotheosis both in
Horace and Virgil. The imaginative powers of the Roman
poets were feeble, and therefore we find in them a constant
falling back upon real life and actual scenes or places, as
well as the above mixture of the divine with the human.
Direct impressions from the external world and actual life
supported even Virgil and Horace, who shew plainly that
they well knew the difficulty of clothing contemporary

history in a poetical dress. Virgil has recourse to the legendary in his descriptions of past history, and to the prophetic shade with which he shrouds his contemporary statements mysteriously. He brings in Evander and Anchises to avoid the prosy dryness and dulness of strict narrative. Horace shrinks from launching his river-boat on the sea—

> Phoebus volentem proelia me loqui
> Victas et urbes increpuit lyra,
> Ne parva Tyrrhenum per aequor
> Vela darem.—*Od.* iv. 15, 1

and lays down imperial history as the subject of the songs which will be popular :

> Virtute functos more patrum duces
> Lydis remixto carmine tibiis
> Trojamque et Anchisen et almae
> Progeniem Veneris canemus.
>
> *Od.* iv. 15, 29.

The poets shewed in this way that they were aware of the prosy tendencies of the national character, and that they must fly for help to ancient times and legendary stories. But the realism of the nation exhibited itself in other unmistakable traits. For instance the similes of Virgil, and still more of the later poets, when compared with those of the great Greek bards, have generally a particular local reference rather than a general. When Virgil compares his defeated heroes to fallen trees, he names a particular spot where the tree was standing. When he compares the habits of the Greeks to flights of birds, the locality whence the birds come is mentioned, and so also in the case of lightning or storms. This tendency corresponds to the exact technical finish, and imitation of actual varieties of shape which a student of Græco-Roman sculpture must have often laid down in his mind as one of its characteristics. Hence we find crowds on the Roman reliefs instead of separate figures or groups. We gather then that the principal influences of Roman character and circumstances upon their art may be roughly stated as follows. First, their innate *severitas* and realism produced satire in poetry, biographic tendencies in history, caricature, technical finish and excessive exactitude in art ; while secondly, their world-wide empire and wealth enlarged and confused both poetry and art, giving rise to a composite style in both, and a preference of quantity to quality, and of crowds to groups. Let us therefore proceed to consider :

I. Roman portrait sculpture.

II. Historical military art in the Roman empire.

III. Composite and colossal art in the same.

IV. Technical finish and luxurious art in the same.

V. Roman architecture, its nationality,

and to indicate how these may be used to shew the general
tendencies of Roman literature and art towards :

1. Ugly portraits.

2. National legends and military hosts.

3. Huge buildings and confused crowds.

4. Finished and sensual details in art.

5. Modifications in architecture.

ESSAY I.

ROMAN PORTRAIT SCULPTURE.

SENECA gives three reasons for the creation of works of art. In the first place he says that such works may be made to be sold and to gain profitable employment; secondly, that the artist may be endeavouring to gain reputation and fame as a man of distinguished ability; and thirdly, that the religious uses of such works are widely extended. To these three Seneca says that Plato would have added a fourth, namely, the realisation of ideal beauty, the imitation of a model as conceived in the mind. And this was no doubt in great measure the origin of the grand models of Greek sculpture. The imaginative power of the Hellenic mind was great enough to realise the idea of abstract perfection in shape, and to employ it in imitations of the human figure. And therefore Phidias and Polycletus soared into a transcendental region, and their fancy fetched

Even from the blazing chariot of the Sun
A beardless youth who touched a golden lute
And filled the illumined groves with ravishment.

MARCUS AGRIPPA.

But the realistic turn of the Roman mind could not appreciate imaginary beauty, and therefore Roman poets and Roman artists contented themselves with exact

CLAUDIUS.

representations of the actual facts and figures of human life, and we find the Roman connoisseurs criticising Polycletus for clothing his statues in superhuman beauty.

D

The Greek artist in executing a portrait statue or bust had the ideal shape before his mind of what the subject of his portrait would be like if all his defective features were corrected and remodelled. This feeling was so strong and active that a Greek artist was admired for what the Romans censured in Polycletus, and was criticised if he produced too literal a representation of any peculiarities in the features of his subject. What the Hellenic mind looked for in a portrait was something beyond the barren pleasure of a likeness. It was the ideal form of which the actual was only the shadow. As Lessing remarks in his *Laocoon*, this feeling was carried to such an extent that the arts were subjected to municipal regulations, recommending the artist to use imitation of nature as a means of arriving at ideal beauty, but prohibiting on pain of punishment its use for producing an exact representation of defects in shape.[1]

ἀπειλεῖ ὁ νόμος Θήβῃσι τοῖς εἰς τὸ χεῖρον πλάσασι ζημίαν τὸ τίμημα δρᾶν.—Ælian. *Var. Hist.* iv. 4.

The Roman characteristic, on the other hand, as shewn in their portrait sculpture and in their literature, is that

---

[1] The law threatens at Thebes that the sculptor who makes his portrait statue worse looking than the original shall suffer a fine to the amount the statue is valued at.

the features and the limbs of those who are represented
are expected to have an exact resemblance, sometimes even
caricature-like, to the original. Thus in their attempts to
imitate form, as in the cases of the portrait busts or statues
of Pompey, Agrippa, and Germanicus, or Claudius (pp. 32,
33), this Roman realism interferes with the shape of the
limbs and spoils the ideal effect. And then the same love
of real and exact imitation afterwards dresses the imperial
and official statues in ornamental cuirasses and belts.

Therefore it may be said that the idea underlying Roman
portrait sculpture was the degradation of the divine to the
human form, and when further developed, would have
generated a fondness for such exhibitions as Madame
Tussaud's Gallery.

Perhaps the word *similitudo* used by Quintilian when
he criticises a sculptor [1]—

Tamquam nimius in veritate Demetrius fuit et similitudinis quam
pulchritudinis amantior.—xii. 10, 9—

is the special characteristic of Roman portrait sculpture.
For we find this aimed at particularly, as was natural, by
the collections of ancestral portraits, and it was an immediate consequence of the spirit in which the Roman

---

[1] Demetrius was too particularly correct, and admired a good
likeness more than a beautiful representation.

worshipped his heroic ancestors. The sculptor under the influence of this Roman spirit did not trust to his ideas of beauty or proportion, but strictly followed what he saw or what he could measure in actual existence.

The idea with which the Romans regarded their portrait statues and busts may be best expressed by the English term idolatry as defined by the Jews, and forbidden in the Ten Commandments, a worship of the exact shape, even of an ugly shape, without any mental idealisation.

The saying of Quintilian about Polycletus is well known as a prediction of one of the dangers into which he saw that the Romans were in danger of falling by avoiding idealisation : [1]

Diligentia ac decor in Polycleto supra ceteros, cui quamquam a plerisque tribuitur palma, tamen, ne nihil detrahatur, deesse pondus putant. Nam ut humanae formae decorem addiderit supra verum, ita non explevisse deorum auctoritatem videtur. Quin aetatem quoque graviorem dicitur refugisse, nihil ausus ultra leves genas.—xii. 10, 9.

Prof. Sellar has remarked upon this stage of Roman history in which devotion to an individual and admiration

---

[1] Though Polycletus excelled all others yet they think he was deficient in gravity. He added beauty to the human form, but did not give the gods an authoritative look. And he is said to have avoided the representation of old people, and to have ventured on nothing but smooth cheeks.

ÆSCHINES.

of him in every respect prevailed (*Roman Poets of the Augustan Age—Virgil*, p. 82): ' As Augustus moulded the policy, Virgil moulded the political feeling of the future.

It is in his poems that loyalty to one man, which soon
became, and till a comparatively recent period continued
to be, the master force in European politics—apparently a
necessary stage in the ultimate evolution of free national
life on a large scale—finds its earliest expression.' And
again, ' Loyalty to a person appealed to the imagination
with the charm of novelty, and might be justified to the
conscience of the world as being, for that time and the
times that came after, the necessary bond of order and
civil union.'

Lysippus was one of the Greek portrait sculptors whose
works were brought to Rome in great numbers. Metellus
brought a number of statues representing Alexander and
his followers at the battle of the Granicus, which afterwards remained in the portico of Octavia.

> Turmam fecit Alexandri, in qua amicorum eius imagines summa
> omnium similitudine expressit ; hanc Metellus Macedonia subacta
> transtulit Romam.—*Nat. Hist.* xxxiv. 64.

Pliny afterwards adds that Lysippus professed his object to
be not to make statues of men as they really were, but as
they appeared to be.

> Volgo dicebat (Lysippus) ab illis factos, quales essent homines, a se,
> quales viderentur esse.—*Id. ib.* 65.

He did not act strictly by measure, but followed the

judgment of his eye as to proportions. His Apoxyomenos is an instance of this, which Agrippa brought from Greece—

Signa fecit inter quæ destringentem se quem Marcus Agrippa ante thermas suas dicavit.—*Nat. Hist.* xxxiv. 62—

and placed in front of his thermæ. This work of Lysippus was most popular at Rome, and no doubt the Greek sculptors employed there imitated its style, which is very pleasing to the eye, though not according to the most natural style of beauty (p. 37).

The erection of statues in honour of famous men at Rome can be traced back by the statements of Pliny, and of Cicero and Livy, to the middle of the fifth century before the Christian era (see J. J. Bernoulli, *Rom. Icon.* i. p. 2), and was therefore anterior to the introduction of Greek portrait statues into Rome. We can also refer to the legal phrase *jus imaginum*, and to the well-known custom of wax images of ancestors set up in the atrium of a Roman house, as proving how familiar such portrait busts or statues were in early times of the Roman national history. That the ancient statues were bearded shews their early date; and the censorial decree ordering all statues which had not been placed in the forum by the state authority to be removed in the year B.C. 158, shews that the number was becoming inconvenient.

Statuas circa forum eorum qni magistratum gesserant sublatas omnes praeter eas quae populi aut senatus sententia statutae essent.—Pliny, *Nat. Hist.* xxxiv. 30.

A first step from the Greek idealisation of nature towards the extreme humanisation of Roman portrait sculpture was taken by Lysippus, who, in his portraits of Alexander and of other heroes, allowed their defects from symmetrical beauty to appear more plainly than the stricter criticism of the national Greek mind would have thought endurable.

He was followed in this by his brother Lysistratus, who, as we are told by Pliny—

Hominis autem imaginem gypso e facie ipsa primus omnium expressit ceraque in eam formam gypsi infusa emendare instituit Lysistratus Sicyonius frater Lysippi, de quo diximus.—*Nat. Hist.* xxxv. 153—

first took casts in gypsum from the faces of those he wished to represent. The idealism became gradually more and more modified by alterations in the hair and in the proportions, and in later times by the introduction of head-dresses, belts, and cuirasses, ornamented historically or biographically. The purpose of the Greek artist in shaping a bust or statue was to make it impressive, while the Roman's purpose was to render it expressive. The Greek wished to impress the mind of the spectator, the

Roman to express the character of the person represented.

The portrait busts of Marius and of Seneca are striking examples of the Roman exaggeration in personal traits of feature. The imperial fiery glance of which Cicero speaks as a characteristic of Marius—

Quodsi vultus C. Marii, si vox, si ille imperatorius ardor oculorum, si recentes triumphi, si praesens valuit adspectus.—*Pro Balbo*. xxi. 49—

and his savage and bitter cast of countenance mentioned by Plutarch—

Μαρίου λιθίνην εἰκόνα πάνυ τῇ λεγομένῃ περὶ τὸ ἦθος στρυφνότητι καὶ πικρίᾳ πρέπουσαν.—*Mar*. ii.—

are unpleasantly reproduced in the heads preserved in the Vatican and in the Munich Glyptothek.

The special interest which the Romans took in the cast of countenance and bodily shape is shewn by numerous passages in the popular writings of the first two centuries B.C. Thus Plutarch, who lived at the end of the first century, in his life of Pompey, begins by speaking of the attractive features which, even in his youth, rendered Pompey a popular speaker, and had something of dignity and princely bearing in them. Plutarch also says that Pompey's hair

and eyes were said to resemble those shewn in the likenesses of Alexander the Great—

ἦν δέ τις καὶ ἀναστολὴ τῆς κόμης ἀτρέμα καὶ τῶν περὶ τὰ ὄμματα ῥυθμῶν
ὑγρότης τοῦ προσώπου ποιοῦσα μᾶλλον λεγομένην ἢ φαινομένην ὁμοιότητα
πρὸς τὰς ᾿Αλεξάνδρου τοῦ βασιλέως εἰκόνας.—*Pomp*. ii.—

but thinks that this was more talked of than really
apparent, shewing that the cast of countenance was often
noticed at Rome in the case of prominent statesmen.

Horace also allows that breath and life are brought back
to the images of great men after their death by public
memorials—

> Non incisa notis marmora publicis,
> Per quæ spiritus et vita redit bonis
> Post mortem ducibus.—*Od*. iv. 8, 13—

and he claims for poetry the same power as for these
memorials:

> Dilecti tibi Virgilius Variusque poetae ;
> Nec magis expressi vultus per aenea signa,
> Quam per vatis opus mores animique virorum
> Clarorum apparent.—*Ep*. ii. 1, 247.

Thus he places the expression of the face on a level with the
character, the one as shown in statues, the other in poetry.
The forehead, as we have seen, is noticed by Roman
writers as a most important feature, and as the part where
honour resided, and by which respect was enforced.   Hence

ANTONIA.

the Roman women, with that curious polarity which often
sets the fashion in exactly the opposite direction to what
would be expected, the Roman women, I say, held that a

narrow forehead with the hair drawn down over it was
pretty and attractive (p. 43).   This may be seen in remaining busts and coins, and is fashionable at the present time.
We have in Horace the terms 'thin,' 'narrow,' 'contracted,' 'confined,' all applied to *frons* as expressive
of beauty (Hor. *Od.* i. 33, 5 ; *Ep.* i. 7, 26 ; *Epod.* xiii. 5 ;
Sat. ii. 2, 125).   This is also noticed by Lucian—

Αἱ μέχρι τῶν ὀφρύων ἐφειλκυσμέναι κόμαι βραχὺ τῷ μετώπῳ τὸ μετ-
αίχμιον ἀφιᾶσι.—*Am.* 40.

But a fine forehead was, on the contrary, considered as a
mark of high character in a Roman hero.   Thus Pliny
uses the expression 'a man of splendid forehead,' and
Lucan in describing the magnificent head of Pompeius
speaks of a 'generous forehead,' and says of the powerful
expression in Pompeius' face,

Hac facie, Fortuna, tibi, Romana placebas.—Lucan, *Phars.* viii. 686.

Virgil shews in his description of personal influence how
much power he attributed to the expression of the countenance.   In the first book of the *Æneid* we have the
almighty look of Jupiter noticed when the storm has been
raised by Æolus, and Venus has persuaded her father to
make it cease,

Vultu, quo caelum tempestatesque serenat.—*Æn.* i. 255.

It is one of the most noble lines of Virgil. Again in the same book we have feelings expressed by a look where Æneas encourages his men by the expression of his face—

> Spem vultu simulat, premit altum corde dolorem.—*Æn.* i. 209 ;

and Dido shews a friendly yet composed and modest welcome to Ilioneus and the Trojan deputation,

> Tum breviter Dido, vultum demissa, profatur.—*Æn.* i. 561.

Cicero appeals to the pose and features of a statue of Scipio,

> Quam esse eiusdem status, amictus, anulus, imago ipsa declarat.— *Ad. Att.* vi. 1, 17 ;

and Seneca admires a calm and honest look :

> Improbum risus, insanum vultus habitusque demonstrat.[1]—*Ep.* 52, 12.
>
> Tertia bona, tamquam modestus incessus et compositus ac probus vultus.—*Ep.* 65, 5.

Lucan lays much stress upon the commanding look of Pompey's face in the well-known line above mentioned, and in the previous lines his hair is spoken of as an object of veneration by kings :

> Illa verenda
> Regibus, hirta coma, et generosa fronte decora
> Cæsaries.—*Phars.* viii. 679.

---

[1] A wicked man betrays himself by his laugh ; a madman is shewn by his countenance and his dress.

CARACALLA.

In the account Lucan gives of Scaeva's bravery shewn by
plucking the arrow from his eye, which is a scene

NERO.

reminding us of a late phase of Greek sculpture in its
horrid details, considerable importance is laid first upon
the mutilation of his face,

Perdiderat vultum rabies ; stetit imbre cruento
Informis facies.—*Phars*. vi. 221 ;

and then upon the composed and mild looks which he
assumes—

Mitis et a vultu penitus virtute remota.—*Phars*. vi. 226—

by which he is said to convince the enemy that he is a
deserter from Cæsar's camp (see pp. 46, 47).

The expression of emotion by the look of the feature,
is of course frequently noticed by all poets ancient and
modern, and it is difficult to say whether Roman poets are
peculiarly remarkable for the epithets which they thus
apply. But a search for the epithets used in Horace or
the other lyrical writers of Rome with the words *vultus*
or *frons* will shew how closely they connected personal
appearance with character. The six epithets, *acer, torvus,
trux, moestus, mutabilis, invitus*, are all applied by Horace
to the expression of the face.

In all of Suetonius's lives of the Cæsars, except that of
Vitellius, we find a particular description of the personal
appearance of the emperor whose life the biographer is
relating. In several cases the shape of the nose and the
appearance of the hair is noticed, and in his account of
Domitian, whose character and personal appearance
were so different, Suetonius records a striking fact.

The emperor says that the Senate approves of his looks—

Commendari se verecundia oris adèo sentiebat, ut apud senatum sic quondam iactaverit : Usque adhuc certe et animum meum probastis et vultum.[1]—Suet. *Dom.* 18—

shewing what importance was attached by the Roman Senate to the appearance of their presidents.   Domitian is called a *calvus Nero* by Juvenal.   The contrast between the Greek idealistic representations and the Roman realism is shewn by Pliny when, in his account of Lysippus, he says that Lysippus used to assert that his object in making a portrait statue was to produce the form which appeared in his own mind, while the ancient sculptors, to whom the Romans went back, tried to make their statues an exact reproduction of the original.

Volgo dicebat ab illis factos, quales essent homines, a se, quales viderentur esse.—Plin. *Nat. Hist.* xxxiv. 65.

The portrait heads of Alexander in the Capitoline Museum at Rome, when compared with that in the Louvre at Paris, are examples of the contrast between the ideal of the Greeks and the actual of the Romans.   In the latter

---

[1] In the senate he once boasted that up to this time they had approved not only of his mind, but of the expression of his face.

E

DOMITIAN.

we have the great king represented by Lysippus with
changes in the form of his neck and eyes intended to
·conceal their defective appearances, while in the former

these parts are not idealised, and the faults in them are actually represented. We find that, as we have said, the Romans carried the natural desire of seeing the actual features and bodily shape of their heroes far beyond the Greeks, by insisting upon the reproductions of each several part of the body exactly as it stood, whether beautiful or not.

The lofty ideality of the statue of Alexander by Lysippus is expressed in some lines given by Plutarch as inscribed on the statue:

Αὐδάσαντι δ' ἔοικεν ὁ χάλκεος εἰς Δία λεύσσων
Γᾶν ὑπ' ἐμοὶ τίθεμαι, Ζεῦ, σὺ δ' Ὄλυμπον ἔχε.

De Fort. Alex. 2.

Yet Lysippus was one of the most realistic of Greek sculptors.

To shew further the importance attached by the Roman people to the busts and statues of their ancestors and men of influence, reference need only be made to some passages in Tacitus. Speaking of the funeral of Germanicus, the historian mentions the complaints of the Roman people that the likeness of Germanicus had not been publicly exhibited according to ancient custom. Hortalus when addressing the Senate is spoken of as appealing to the statues:

Modo Hortensii inter oratores sitam imaginem, modo Augusti intuens.—*Ann.* ii. 37.

AUGUSTUS.

Again the sale of a statue of Augustus with the other ornaments of his gardens was brought forward as a special accusation against Falanius. One of the signs of the greatest hatred and contempt at Rome was that a man's bust should be dragged to the Gemonian steps and destroyed, and in token of the restoration to favour of Poppæa, and even of Nero, their statues were to be restored. The accusation of treason against Granius Marcellus contained this point, that he had placed his own statue higher than that of Cæsar.

One of the honours which generally accompanied a triumph was that a *statua triumphalis* should be granted, and a number of these statues stood in the Forum at Rome :

Tigellinum et Nervam ita extollens, ut super triumphales in foro imagines apud Palatinum quoque effigies eorum sisteret. — *Ann.* xv. 72.

In his description of the last moments of Vitellius, Tacitus mentions the falling statues as one of the signs of his fall which Vitellius beheld. Thus the Romans deified the bodies of their heroes.

The characters of the two Agrippinas as drawn by Tacitus are expressed in the busts which we have in the Capitol at Rome. In the one we see the pure dignified heroic lady ; in the other, the desperate, ambitious, but unhappy mother. Of the elder Agrippina we have the picture in the extract from Tacitus on the next page :

AGRIPPINA.

Femina ingens animi munia ducis per eos dies induit militibusque,
ut quis inops aut saucius, vestem et fomenta dilargita est.   Tradit C.
Plinius stetisse apud principium pontis, laudes et grates reversis
legionibus habentem.—*Ann.* i. 69.

ROMAN LADY.

Of the younger, her interview with her son Nero is described most vividly, and her power not of argument but of look :

Colloquium filii exposcit, ubi nihil pro innocentia, quasi diffideret, nec beneficiis, quasi exprobraret disseruit, sed ultionem in delatores et praemia amicis obtinuit.—*Ann.* xiii. 21.

The value attached by the Romans to the expressions of the face as an index of the feelings of the mind is shewn by some statements of Pliny and Quintilian. The former of these writers says of the forehead :

Frons et aliis sed homini tantum tristitiae, hilaritatis, clementiae, severitatis index, in animo sensus eius. Superbia aliubi conceptaculum, sed hic sedem habet, in corde nascitur, huc subit, hic pendet.— *Nat. Hist.* xi. 51.

And again he speaks of the eye, and of the nose and their power :

Profecto in oculis animus habitat : ardent, intenduntur, umectant, connivent.—*Nat. Hist.* xi. 54.

Inter eas (malas) hilaritatem risumque indicantes buccae, et altior homini tantum, quem novi mores subdolae inrisioni dicavere, nasus. —Id. *ib.* 59.

Pliny also speaks of the Roman names, such as Pætus, Strabo, Silus, Cocles, and others which are taken from the shape of the face and appearance of the eyes and nose.

The expressions of the face are spoken of by Quintilian in a way which shews that the Roman rhetorical schools,

VESPASIAN.

as we should naturally expect, attached much importance to them:

Nam frons pluribus generibus peccat. Vidi multos quorum super-
cilia ad singulos vocis conatus allevarentur, aliorum constricta, aliorum
etiam dissidentia, cum altero in verticem tenderent, altero paene oculus
ipse premertur.—*Inst. Or.* i. 11, 10.

In the eleventh book of his *Institutio Oratoria* Quintilian
lays down rules for the proper management of the face in
oratory, which he treats together with the action of the
head, arms, and other parts of the body :

Multum et superciliis agitur. Nam et oculos formant aliquatenus
et fronti imperant. His contrahitur, attollitur, demittitur.—*Inst. Or.*
xi. 3, 78.

Then he goes on to speak of the various affections of the
mind indicated by the brow :

Ira enim contractis, tristitia deductis, hilaritas remissis ostenditur.
—Id. *ib.* 79.

Cicero in his *De Natura Deorum* rises above his fellow-
countrymen, as he generally does.   Speaking as a student
of Greek philosophy, in his observations on the appearance
of the gods, he says,

Redeo ad Deos. Ecquos si non tam strabones at paetulos esse arbi-
tramur? ecquos naevum habere? ecquos silos flaccos, frontones, capi-
tones quae sunt in nobis ?[1]—*De Nat. Deor.* i. 29, § 80.

---

[1] To return to the subject of the gods. Are we to think that
there are any of them, I won't say squinting, but with a cast in
the eyes ?   That any of them have warts, or are snub-nosed, or
flap-eared, or have large foreheads or heads, like men ?

NERVA.

that the defects of the human face cannot be attributed
to the divine face, that among the gods there are no snub-
nosed or squinting gods, thus idealising the divine form.

He follows the Greek idea of divinity as far above all
human feeling or expression of human defects.

Catullus has expressed but little Roman patriotism in
his poetry. His strong republican feeling does not lead
him to hero-worship but rather to political satire, as in his
attacks upon Julius Caesar and Mamurra. Of them
Catullus says many fiercely severe things :

> Nil nimium studeo, Caesar, tibi velle placere,
>   Nec scire utrum sis albus an ater homo.
> > *Carm.* xciii.

The Roman love of the degradation of art into caricature
did not appear in many of his satires. But some, it must
be said, are striking caricatures, as that of Egnatius :

> Egnatius quod candidos habet dentes
> Renidet usquequaque.—*Id.* xxxix.

and his remarks upon the ugly nose of a girl he dislikes,

> Ista turpiculo puella naso.—*Id.* xli.
>   nec minimo puella naso.—*Id.* xliii.

and the lovely eyes of a boy,

> Mellitos oculos tuos, Juventi,
> Si quis me sinat usque basiare.—*Id.* xlviii.

shew that Catullus drew a strong feeling from the features
of those he liked or disliked.

CALIGULA.

Further developments of the tendency to describe the
personal characteristics of individuals can be traced, as
might be expected, in the satirists. Persius makes use of

expressive indications of the nose, the ears, and the complexion :

> Ira cadat naso rugosaque sanna.—Pers. v. 91.
> Ingeminat tremulos naso crispante cachinnos.—iii. 87.
> Auriculas asini Mida rex habet ?—i. 121.

In the famous lines in his fifth book, the contour of a man's face and complexion are noticed as expressive :

> At te nocturnis juvat impallescere chartis.
> Cultor enim iuvenum purgatas inseris aures
> Fruge Cleanthea.—*Id.* v. 62.

The formation of mental habits is compared by him to the moulding of the features of the face by a sculptor.

> Artificemque tuo ducit sub pollice vultum.—v. 40.

Juvenal constantly makes the features and the personal peculiarities of those he alludes to a means of illustrating their character and moral qualities. So Domitian is called 'a bald Nero' by him, as he is also by Ausonius. Their meaning is to call Domitian a Nero in every vice, excepting only that he has one feature which Nero had not got, and which ought to have shewn that he was serious and experienced, but unfortunately indicates that he is growing old in crime.

Some of the most striking passages in Juvenal are his descriptions of Sejanus and Hannibal, in both of which he

remarks on the shew of character in the countenance.
The lines on Sejanus in the tenth satire are well known,
where he remarks on the life and the look of Sejanus:

> Seianus ducitur unco
> Spectandus: gaudent omnes.   Quae labra ! quis illi
> Vultus erat !—*Sat.* x. 66.

But it is difficult to be certain whether the prevailing
notion in Juvenal's mind when he wrote the description
of Hannibal—

> O qualis facies et quali digna tabella,
> Cum Gaetula ducem portaret bellua luscum.
> *Sat.* x. 157—

was intended to picture the great general at the height of
his glory, or to caricature him as already beginning to
suffer under the reverses which were afterwards to befall
him, and which the satirist goes on to describe.   Probably
Juvenal holds up the picture of Hannibal's lost eye as
portending his approaching downfall.   The frown of dis-
satisfaction as spoken of by Juvenal and Seneca was so
natural to the human face, that it can hardly be spoken of
as peculiarly Roman.   In two passages of his Satires—

> Si rugam trahit extenditque labellum.
> *Sat.* xiv. 325.
> Densissima ruga
> Cogitur in frontem.—*Id. Sat.* xiii. 215—

Juvenal speaks of the wrinkled brow not as a sign of old age, which is usual, but as a mark by which a man's countenance exhibits displeasure. In the former of these passages he adds, 'and extends his lips,' a phrase which may have the meaning of protruding the lip or lengthening it, the former of which seems to indicate scorn, while the latter shows astonishment.

The shape of the body is certainly connected with the qualities of the mind by Juvenal, when he derides Montanus,

> Montani quoque venter adest abdomine tardus.
>
> *Sat.* iv. 107,

and criticises Lateranus,

> pinguis Lateranus.—Id. *ib.* viii. 147.

A connection between personal appearance and character was much believed in by the Romans, as is shewn, besides the poetry above quoted, by numerous passages in their prose literature. We have elsewhere remarked that the statue of a distinguished person was surveyed by them with the same emotions which they felt towards the real person himself, and the national custom of placing the representations of their ancestors in the court of the family mansion is well known to all students of Roman history. The right of having likenesses was a department of their

SEVERUS.

huge legal system. Becker (*Hdbk.* ii. 1, p. 220) gives a
number of passages from different writers on this subject,
which shew that some of these likenesses were on statues,

F

and others giv$n in printed fresco likenesses. At the funeral of Drusus we read in Tacitus that a long procession of likenesses was carried,

Funus imaginum pompa maxime illustre fuit, cum origo Iuliae gentis Aeneas omnesque Albanorum reges et conditor urbis Romulus, post Sabina nobilitas, Attus Clausus ceteraeque Claudiorum effigies longo ordine spectarentur.—*Ann.* iv. 9.

Livy says that outside the porta Capena, at the monument of the Scipio family, were three statues, two of which represented Publius and Lucius Scipio, and the other the poet Ennius :

Prohibuisse (Scipionem) ne decerneretur ut imago sua triumphali ornatu e templo Jovis optimi maximi exiret.—xxxviii. 56.

Romae extra portam Capenam in Scipionem monumento tres statuae sunt, duae P. et L. Scipionum, tertia poetae Q. Ennii.—xxxviii. 56.

to which he evidently alludes as facts of historical importance. Also that Scipio refused to allow his statue to be worshipped or introduced into a temple. Plutarch appeals to the statues of Romulus at Rome as evidence proving that Dionysius was wrong in saying that Romulus used a chariot in his triumphal procession :

Τοῦ δὲ ῾Ρωμύλου τὰς εἰκόνας ὁρᾶν ἔστιν ἐν ῾Ρώμῃ τὰς ρροπαιοφόρους πεζὰς ἁπάσας.—Plut. *Rom.* 16.

In his *Natural History* Pliny speaks of the strong influence statues had on the Roman mind, and distinctly asserts that the expression on the face is a peculiarity of the human race :

Facies homini tantum, ceteris os aut rostra.—*Nat. Hist.* xi. 51.

He also gives credit to the liberality of the Romans in permitting statues of Hannibal to stand in three places at Rome :

Adeo discrimen omne sublatum est, ut Hannibalis etiam statuae tribus locis visantur.—*Nat. Hist.* xxxiv. 6, 15.

ESSAY II.

NATIONAL AND HISTORICAL TENDENCY.

THE influence upon art of the Roman national pride appears very distinctly in numerous medallions.[1] We have on medallions of the age of the Antonines scenes representing the reception of Hercules by Evander, and the sow with her thirty young pigs, celebrated in the third Æneid as marking the place where Rome was to be built :

> Cum tibi sollicito secreti ad fluminis undam
> Litoreis ingens inventa sub ilicibus sus
> Triginta capitum fetus enixa iacebit,
> Alba, solo recubans, albi circum ubera nati ;
> Is locus urbis erit, requies ea certa laborum.
> > *Æn.* iii. 389.

We also have Æneas carrying his father away from Troy, and Horatius Cocles swimming over the Tiber after cutting

---

[1] See W. Froehner's *Medallions Romains*, p. 57.

down the Sublician Bridge. All these shew how the art of the poet and designer of coins were affected by the national historical spirit of the Romans.

WOLF AND TWINS.

The pride of the Romans in their early history is displayed on the reverses of many medallions, where we have the figures of the early Roman legendary history, such as the wolf and twins, Anchises and Æneas,

Their martial pride also shews itself in the great number of reverses on medallions commemorating their victories by the titles of *triumphator* or *victoria* with many others. Pride in their great metropolitan centre appears in the figures of Rome. But we must not deny them the credit of exalting high moral qualities such as those of *Pietas, Virtus, Pudicitia, Liberalitas, Fides,* which appear constantly on medallions and in their poetry, as often as the more imperial titles of *Securitas, Fecunditas, Gaudium, Gloria,* and one which shews their confidence in wealth, *Moneta.*[1]

The national historical element which prevailed so largely in Roman epic poetry was introduced, so far as we know, by Nævius, when he wrote a poem on the first Punic war in Saturnian metre. From the fragments and notices in Servius which we have left us of the first and second books of this Epic poem, we conclude that he began by a description of the foundation and growth of Rome and Carthage :

> Qui terrai Latiai hemones tuserunt
> Vires frudesque Pœnicas fabor.[2]
>> Nævius, *De Bello Punico I.* (Klussmaen).

---

[1] See Froehner's *Medallions Romains,* and many passages in Statius.
[2] I shall speak of the men who violently attacked the land of Latium, the strong and wily Carthaginians.

Nævius appears to have connected the two cities Rome and Carthage together in the same way as Virgil did afterwards by taking Æneas to Africa, and involving him there in intercourse with the foundress of Carthage. We find also in Nævius the same connection of Rome with divine and heroic beings which was used by Virgil to give a high and mysterious tone to the *Æneid*. The Penates and Anchises appear, and are backed up by the Pythian Apollo and the Eleusinian deities. Thus Nævius began the endeavour of Roman poetry to shroud contemporary history in a mythical veil and give it a romantic aspect.

Professor Sellar (*Roman Poets of the Augustan Age— Virgil*, p. 79), speaking of Virgil's national feeling, quotes the French writers Coulanges and Patin as follows : ' Dans ce poème,' writes M. Coulanges of the *Æneid*, ' ils les Romains se voyaient, eux, leur fondateur, leur ville, les in-stitutions, leurs croyances, leur Empire.'   M. Patin, again, describes the same poem as 'expression de Rome, de Rome entière, de la Rome de tous les temps, de celle des Empereurs, des Consuls, des Rois.'

Virgil was by far more national a poet than Horace, who says that it is absurd to identify the Alban mount with Olympus, and to make it the abode of the Muses, and derides those who do so :

Pontificum libros, annosa volumina vatum,
Dictitet Albano Musas in monte locutas.

Hor. *Ep.* ii. 1. 27.

M. Boissier, in speaking of Virgil's love for Italy, and his identification of the Greek legends with the Roman, says, ' On voit pourtant qu'il a cherché à conserver de quelque façon à sa mythologie un caractère national, et c'est là son originalité parmi les poètes de son pays. D'abord, il est visible que lorsqu'il emprunte une fable aux poètes grecs, il s'efforce d'en placer le théâtre dans quelque coin de la terre italienne' : so in the following passages—

Insula Sicanium juxta latus Aeoliamque
Erigitur Liparen, fumantibus ardua saxis,
Quam subter specus et Cyclopum exesa caminis
Antra Aetnaea tonant   *   *
        *   *   *   *
Volcani domus et Volcania nomine tellus.

Æn. viii. 416.

Est locus Italiae medio sub montibus altis,
Nobilis et fama multis memoratus in oris,
Amsancti valles   *   *
Hic specus horrendum et saevi spiracula Ditis
Monstrantur, ruptoque ingens Acheronte vorago
Pestiferas aperit fauces.—*Æn.* vii. 563.

And hence we have in the *Æneid* two long processional pictures, one, in the first book, of the early legendary history beginning with Æneas and Ascanius, and ascending through the Alban dynasty to Romulus and finally to Cæsar himself; the other, in the sixth book, where Anchises reviews the kings and warriors of the nation, not passing over even the republican heroes, Cato, Fabricius, and the Fabii. Such glorifications, more or less adulatory of Roman national exploits and of national military magnificence, became afterwards one of the principal features of the Roman Epic. Roman art both in poetry and in sculpture sacrificed, as we shall see, beauty to national pride in detailing events, and thus poetry was marred by the tedious and prosaic narratives we find in *Silius Italicus*, and art by the long processional and nationalistic reliefs of the triumphal arches, and by the imitation of works belonging to the later Greek sculpture, such as the Toro Farnese and the Laocoon.

Lucilius besides his patriotic admiration of the statesmen and generals of his own time connects the early history of Rome in the first book of his *Satires* with the councils of the gods :

Consilium summis hominum de rebus habebant.—I. 6. (Müller).

He afterwards explains that the highest subject of human interest to which the gods are giving their attention is the prosperity of the Roman state,

Quo populum adque urbem pacto servare potissit
Ampliu' Romanam ?—Lucil. 1. xiii.

His lines might almost be taken as a statement of the
subject of Virgil's *Æneid*.

By such a union of the national with the celestial,
the early and the Augustan age of Roman poetry and
art may be said to have resembled the Periclean age in
Greece, but it must also be added that the Roman was
less cosmopolitan and more exclusively national than
the Greek.

Ennius was led by the same enthusiastic national feeling
as Nævius and Virgil into making the subject of his epic
a narrative of Roman history. Thus he wrote in entire
harmony with the patriotic feeling of his countrymen, but
could not rise from the battlefield into the higher imaginative regions into which Homer soared. The Trojan origin
of Rome is used by him to connect the national history
with divine sources, and we have the personages of Æneas
and Anchises associated with the Olympic deities, from
whom we descend to the kings and heroes—

Flos delibatus populi suadaeque medulla.—309 (Vahlen)—

as he calls them. The celebrated lines on Fabius
Cunctator—

> Unus homo nobis cunctando restituit rem,
> Noenum rumores ponebat ante salutem.
> Ergo plusque magisque viri nunc gloria claret.—313 ;

and on the friend with whom Servilius took counsel—

> Suavis homo facundus suo contentus beatus
> Scitus secunda loquens in tempore commodus verbum
> Paucum.—350

—belong to this feature of the great poem of Ennius, when he has come down to the natural Roman level of national hero worship.

But the greater part of the Ennian like the later Epic was probably prosaic and lifeless. The series of actions must have had a dull similarity and produced a confused and tedious effect upon the readers. So we have a catalogue-like enumeration of the warlike races of Central Italy—

> Marsa manus, Peligna cohors, Vestina virum vis.
> *Ann.* viii. 280—

which is destitute of the charm given to them by Virgil's harmoniously neat phrases and apt allusions at the end of the seventh book of his *Æneid*. The genius of Ennius was therefore truly Roman, devoid of all imaginative description and supporting itself upon the facts of history, coloured with the pride of national glory.

The same national mode of exalting history appears in the lesser arts as well as in poetry. We have spoken of medallions, and when we look at some of the best engraved

TRIUMPH OF TIBERIUS.

stones which have been preserved, as the sardonyx cameo of Vienna, we find the same mixture of deities and deified heroes. Augustus is seated by the side of Roma and crowned by Cybele. Germanicus and Tiberius figure in front, while we have the usual assemblage of troops and captives below. And again upon the well-known statue of Augustus, gods, Roman mythological beings and soldiers with captives are represented on the emperor's cuirass.

In Lucretius' great poem we have the Roman military power vividly expressed in one or two passages, as the descriptions in the second book, 40 and 323—

> Si non forte tuas legiones per loca campi
> Fervere cum videas, belli simulacra cientis.
> > *De Rer. Nat.* ii. o.4 ;
> Praeterea magnae legiones cum loca cursu
> Camporum complent, belli simulacra cientes.
> > Id. *ib.* 323—

where the extent of the space covered by the legions and the cavalry is the main point of the passage, because the poet wishes to remark upon the diminution of such vast crowds to a mere speck when seen from a distance.

But with the exception of the above passage, and two or three others—

> Ad confligendum venientibus undique Poenis,
> Omnia cum belli trepido concussa tumultu
> Horrida contremuere sub altis aetheris oris.
> > *De Rer. Nat.* iii. 833
> Inde boves lucas turrito corpore taetras,
> Auguimanos, belli docuerunt volnera Poeni
> Sufferre.—*Id.* v. 1301—

SCENE IN FORUM.

where Lucretius speaks of the grandeur and pomp of war, and of the use of elephants as a striking feature, he does not dwell upon the power and conquering grandeur of the Roman nation. As Professor Sellar has remarked, the power of nature in Lucretius takes the place of the power of Rome in Virgil and Horace.

Nor do we find in him the hero-worship of the other Roman poets, for with the exception of the Scipios—

> Scipiadas, belli fulmen, Carthaginis horror.
> *De Rer. Nat.* iii. 1047—

the great warriors of Rome are not mentioned with special distinction. And his martial descriptions are probably derived from Ennius, as they do not refer to the army of his own time but go back to the Punic wars.

The Roman's love for the national military history of his great country which, as we have said, is one of the dominant tones resounding throughout the poems of Nævius, Ennius, and Virgil, is echoed in the writings of the great elegiac poets of Rome.

Thus Tibullus fills one of the longer elegies of his second book with allusions to Æneas and the Laurentian legends, and the early deities of Rome, the Lares and Penates:

> Haec (Sibylla) dedit Aeneae sortes, postquam illa parentem
> Dicitur et raptos sustinuisse Lares,

Nec fore credebat Romam cum maestus ab alto
    Ilion ardentes respiceretque deos. . . . .
Impiger Aenea, volitantis frater Amoris,
    Troica qui profugis sacra vehis ratibus,
Iam tibi Laurentes assignat Iupiter agros ;
    Iam vocat errantes hospita terra Lares.
Illic sanctus eris, cum te veneranda Numici
    Unda deum caelo miserit indigetem.
Ecce super fessas volitat victoria puppes ;
    Tandem ad Troianos diva superba venit.
Ecce mihi lucent Rutulis incendia castris :
    Iam tibi praedico, barbare Turne, necem.
Ante oculos Laurens castrum, murusque Lavini est,
    Albaque ab Ascanio condita Longa duce.
Te quoque iam video, Marti placitura sacerdos,
    Ilia, Vestales deseruisse focos ; . . . .
Carpite nunc, tauri, de septem montibus herbas,
    Dum licet ; hic magnae iam locus urbis erit.
Roma, tuum nomen terris fatale regendis,
    Qua sua de caelo prospicit arva Ceres.
Quaque patent ortus, et qua fluitantibus undis
    Solis anhelantes abluit amnis equos.
Troia quidem tunc se mirabitur, et sibi dicet
    Vos bene tam longa consuluisse via.—Tibul. ii. 5.

Several poems in the fifth book of the elegiac odes of
Propertius are filled in the same way with the historical
legends of early Rome, and have been supposed to be an
incipient attempt to write a *Fasti* like that of Ovid. Of
these the first, second, eighth, and ninth poems are the
most remarkable :

Hoc, quodcumque vides, hospes, qua maxima Roma est,
  Ante Phrygem Aenean collis et herba fuit ;
Atque ubi navali stant sacra Palatia Phoebo,
  Evandri profugae concubuere boves.
Fictilibus crevere deis haec aurea templa :
  Nec fuit opprobrio facta sine arte casa.
Tarpeiusque pater nuda de rupe tonabat,
  Et Tiberis nostris advena bubus erat.
Qua gradibus domus ista Remi se sustulit, olim
  Unus erat fratrum maxima regna focus.
Curia praetexto quae nunc nitet alta Senatu,
  Pellitos habuit, rustica corda, patres.
Buccina cogebat priscos ad verba Quirites ;
  Centum illi in prato saepe Senatus erat.
Nec sinuosa cavo pendebant vela theatro :
  Pulpita solennes non oluere crocos.
Nulli cura fuit externos quaerere divos,
  Cum tremeret patrio pendula turba sacro.

      *   *   *   *   *

Prima galeritus posuit praetoria Lycmon ;
  Magnaque pars Tatio rerum erat inter oves.
Hinc Titiens Ramnesque viri, Luceresque coloni,
  Quatuor hinc albos Romulus egit equos.
Quippe suburbanae parva minus urbe Bovillae.
  Et, qui nunc nulli, maxima turba Gabi.
Et stetit Alba potens, albae suis omine nata,
  Hac ubi Fidenas longa erat ire via.
Nil patrium, nisi nomen, habet Romanus alumnus :
  Sanguinis altricem non pudet esse lupam.—Propert. v. 1.

And again at the beginning and end of the ninth poem
in the fifth book :

                                   G

> Amphytrioniades qua tempestate invencos
>   Egerat a stabulis, o Erythraea, tuis
> Venit ad invictos pecorosa Palatia montes,
>   Et statuit fessos, fessus et ipse, boves ;
> Qua Velabra suo stagnabant flumine, quaque,
>   Nauta per urbanas velificabat aquas.
>
> *   *   *   *   *
>
> Angulus hic mundi nunc me mea fata trahentem
>   Accipit ; haec fesso vix mihi terra patet.
> Maxima quae gregibus devota est ara repertis,
>   Ara per has, inquit, maxima facta manus,
> Haec nullis unquam pateat veneranda puellis,
>   Herculis eximii ne sit inulta sitis.—v. ix.

When we pass on to Juvenal, he has some magnificent passages on the past history of Rome and the military grandeur of the great national heroes,

> Quorum Flaminia tegitur cinis atque Latina.—*Sat.* i. 171.

He derides the pride of the great Roman nobles in their genealogical rolls, and their display of the busts of great ancestors. The famous lines at the beginning of his eighth satire—

> Stemmata quid faciunt? quid prodest, Pontice, longo
> Sanguine censeri pictosque ostendere vultus
> Maiorum, et stantes in curribus Aemilianos,
> Et Curios iam dimidios, umerosque minorem
> Corvinum, et Galbam auriculis nasoque carentem ?
> Quis fructus generis tabula jactare capaci

FAMILY OF CÆSARS.

(Corvinum, posthac multa contingere virga)
Fumosos equitum cum dictatore magistros,
Si coram Lepidis male vivitur? effigies quo
Tot bellatorum, si luditur alea pernox

G 2

Ante Numantimos?   Si dormire incipis ortu
Luciferi, quo signa duces et castra movebant?
Cur Allobrogicis et magna gaudeat ara
Natus in Herculeo Fabius lare, si cupidus, si
Vanus et Euganea quantumvis mollior agna :
Si tenerum attritus Catinensi pumice lumbum
Squalentes traducit avos emptorque veneni
Frangenda miseram funestat imagine gentem ?
Tota licet veteres exornent undique cerae
Atria, nobilitas sola est atque unica virtus.

Sat. viii. 1—

and many other passages shew how military pride
prompted the Romans to fill their houses with works of
art in memory of their remote ancestors, and how the
spoils of war—

Bellorum exuviae . . . .
Humanis maiora bonis creduntur.—*Sat.* x. 133—

were believed to be the most valuable of all possessions.[1]
Then Polybius after describing (Lib. vi. 53, 10) the cere-
monial of a Roman noble's funeral, and the exhibition of
the busts of those in his family who had distinguished
themselves, concludes with remarkable words :

τί δ᾽ ἂν κάλλιον θέαμα τούτου φανείη ;—vi. 53.[2]

---

[1] The spoils of war are believed to be the best of all things.
[2] What sight could be finer than this !

But the historian does not of course add the philosophical criticisms of a satirist.

That Rome was filled, as some of our continental capitals are, with military, is shewn by the fact that the rough spirit of the Roman army is treated as a well-known topic by Persius, who brings before our minds the opinion of the *varicosi centuriones* laughing at Stoic doctrines, or the pursuit of any peaceful occupation,

> Dixeris haec inter varicosos centuriones ;
> Continuo crassum ridet Pulfennius ingens,
> Et centum Graecos curto centusse licetur.
> *Sat.* v. 189.[1]

An admirable illustration may be found also in the sixth *Satire* of Persius of the fondness of the whole Roman people from the empress downwards for military display, and of the realistic nature of the representations carried in a triumph. The empress contracts for pictures or images of the conquered nations, and even of their rivers and territories,

> Essedaque ingentesque locat Caesonia Rhenos.
> *Sat.* vi. 47.

---

[1] Talk thus among the military men with their huge legs, that great overgrown Pulfennius breaks into a horse laugh in your face, and offers a clipped centussis for a lot of a hundred Greeks.

With this passage Jahn has aptly compared one from Ovid
where he speaks of the carriage in procession of pictures
representing mountains and rivers,

> Quae loca, qui montes, quaeve ferantur aquae.
>
> *Ar. Am.* i. 220.[1]

Trajan's column must of course be here mentioned, where,
as Wordsworth says,

> ' Historic figures round the shaft embost
> Ascend with lineaments in air not lost.'
>
> *   *   *   *
>
> ' In every Roman through all turns of fate
> Is Roman dignity inviolate.'
>
> *Miscellaneous Sonnets*, xxv.

This wonderful spiral frieze is truly one of Rome's most
characteristic works. It is criticised by Sir J. Reynolds
as follows :

"But here the sculptor, not content with successful
imitation, if it may be so called, proceeds to represent
figures, or groups of figures, on different planes, that is,
some on the foreground and some at a greater distance, in
the manner of painters in historical compositions. To do
this he has no other means than by making the distant

---

[1] What are those countries they are carrying in the triumph, what
mountains, and what seas ?

figures of less dimensions, and relieving them in a less degree from the surface; but this is not adequate to the end; they will still appear only as figures on a less scale, but equally near the eye with those in front of the piece.

NILE.

"Nor does the mischief of this attempt, which never accomplishes its intention, rest here: by this division of the work into many minute parts, the grandeur of its general effect is inevitably destroyed."

To this may be added a passage from the *Annals* of

Tacitus, ii. 41, where the triumph of Germanicus is described :

Vecta spolia, captivi, simulacra montium, fluminum, proeliorum ; augebat intuentium visus eximia ipsius species currusque quinque liberis onustus.—*Ann.* ii. 41.

And another from the *Natural History* of Pliny, where he says that in the triumph of Balbus—

Dicebatur praeter Cydamum et Garamam omnium aliarum gentium urbiumque nomina ac simulacra duxisse, quae iere hoc ordine.—*Nat. Hist.* v. 5, 5—

the representations of captured nations and towns were carried, and then he gives a long list of captured nations and towns.   Trees were even exhibited—

A Pompeio Magno in triumpho arbores quoque duximus.—*Nat. Hist.* xii. 25, 54.[1]

The Greeks in their national triumphant reliefs represented their victories under the guise of mythical exploits.   The Æacidæ are used in this way in the pedimental groups of the temple of Athene at Ægina, now preserved at Munich.[2] So also in the temple of Zeus at Olympia, and that

---

[1] We carried trees along in the triumphal procession of Pompeius.
[2] Perry's *Catalogue*, No. 48.

ANTONINE APOTHEOSIS.

of Theseus at Athens, battles are represented by Gods and Giants, Centaurs and Lapiths.[1]   But the Romans preferred the real to the ideal, and in consequence they became matter of fact in their triumphal reliefs.

At the beginning of the third book of the *Georgics*, Virgil evidently has the reliefs which the Romans placed on their triumphal arches in his mind, when he enumerates a long line of figures decorating the temple which he imagines himself as dedicating to Augustus. Indian tribes, Egyptian, Asian, and Parthian subdued captives, are marshalled before us. These all represent contemporary history. There is also a group of statues representing the legendary heroes of early Rome and their tutelary deity Apollo. Finally a symbolical statue of repulsed Envy completes the triumphal representation of the grand world-wide power of the emperor. The temple which Dido in the *Æneid* erects is ornamented with paintings which represent the subjects to which the Romans dedicated their artistic powers, namely, the battles between Greeks and Trojans in the plains around Troy ; and scenes are introduced which shew that the taste of the poet was superior to the usual fondness of the Roman for disgusting contemporary horrors and bloodshed :

---

[1] Perry's *Catalogue*, Nos. 76 and 84.

Miratur, videt Iliacas ex ordine pugnas
Bellaque iam fama totum volgata per orbem,
Atridas, Priamumque, et saevum ambobus Achillem.
Constitit, et lacrimans, Quis iam locus, inquit, Achate,
Quae regio in terris nostri non plena laboris ?
En Priamus.   Sunt hic etiam sua praemia laudi ;
Sunt lacrimae rerum et mentem mortalia tangunt.
Solve metus ; feret haec aliquam tibi fama salutem.
Sic ait, atque animum pictura pascit inani,
Multa gemens, largoque humectat flumine vultum.
Namque videbat, uti bellantes Pergama circum
Hac fugerent Graii, premeret Troiana juventus ;
Hac Phryges, instaret curru cristatus Achilles.
Nec procul hinc Rhesi niveis tentoria velis
Agnoscit lacrimans, primo quae prodita somno
Tydides multa vastabat caede cruentus,
Ardentesque avertit equos in castra, prius quam
Pabula gustassent Troiae Xanthumque bibissent.
Parte alia fugiens amissis Troilus armis,
Infelix puer atque impar congressus Achilli,
Fertur equis, curruque haeret resupinus inani,
Lora tenens tamen : huic cervixque comaeque trahuntur
Per terram, et versa pulvis inscribitur hasta.
Interea ad templum non aequae Palladis ibant
Crinibus Iliades passis peplumque ferebant,
Suppliciter tristes et tunsae pectora palmis ;
Diva solo fixos oculos aversa tenebat.
Ter circum Iliacos raptaverat Hectora muros,
Exanimumque auro corpus vendebat Achilles.
Tum vero ingentem gemitum dat pectore ab imo,
Ut spolia, ut currus, utque ipsum corpus amici,
Tendentemque manus Priamum conspexit inermes.
Se quoque principibus permixtum agnoscit Achivis,

Eoasque acies et nigri Memnonis arma.
Ducit Amazonidum lunatis agmina peltis
Penthesilea furens, mediisque in millibus ardet,
Aurea subnectens exsertae cingula mammae,
Bellatrix, audetque viris concurrere virgo.[1]—*Æn.* i. 456—493.

The description of the shield of Æneas in *Æn.* viii. must of course be mentioned as peculiarly illustrative of the Roman historical and military spirit. Homer's shield of Achilles, from which Virgil no doubt took his idea, includes a general picture of the world and of human life. The poet begins with heaven and earth:

Ἐν μὲν γαῖαν ἔτευξ᾽, ἐν δ᾽ οὐρανὸν, ἐν δε θάλασσαν,

and then civil and military life are introduced—civil in a city,

λαοὶ δ᾽ εἰν ἀγορῇ ἔσαν ἀθρόοι· ἔνθα δὲ νεῖκος
ὠρώρει,

and military outside a city,

στησάμενοι δ᾽ ἐμάχοντο μάχην ποταμοῖο παρ᾽ ὄχθας,
βάλλον δ᾽ ἀλλήλους χαλκήρεσιν ἐγχείῃσιν.

After these he proceeds to rural life—first agricultural,

Ἐν δ᾽ ἐτίθει τέμενος βαθυλήιον· ἔνθα δ᾽ ἔριθοι
ἤμων, ὀξείας δρεπάνας ἐν χερσὶν ἔχοντες,

---

[1] He sees there too Penthesilea in her fury leading the Amazons: how she rages in the midst of her soldiers, and though a girl dares to meet men.

and then pastoral,

Ἐν δ' ἀγέλην ποίησε βοῶν ὀρθοκραιράων,

and festal

Ἐν δὲ χορὸν ποίκιλλε.—*Il.* xviii. 483.

Virgil's decorations on the shield of Æneas are all Roman and historical, reminding us more of the triumphal arches at Rome, or of Livy's legendary style, or of Trajan's column than of the noble spiritual power shewn in the best Greek art.

Virgil's groups are probably taken from Roman national sculpture.   He has that famous group of the wolf and twins:[1]

> Fecerat et viridi fetam Mavortis in antro
> Procubuisse lupam; geminos huic ubera circum
> Ludere pendentes pueros, et lambere matrem
> Inpavidos; illam tereti cervice reflexam
> Mulcere alternos, et corpora fingere lingua—

and then such as we find on triumphal arches—whether an imperial statue—

> Hinc Augustus agens Italos in proelia Caesar
> Cum Patribus Populoque, Penatibus et magnis Dis,
> Stans celsa in puppi—

---

[1] Virg. *Æn.* ix. 642.   The wolf and the twins.   The highest law is that all coming wars will be crushed under the feet of the family of Assaracus.

or a submissive power—

> Contra autem magno moerentem corpore Nilum,
> Pandentemque sinus et tota veste vocantem
> Caeruleum in gremium latebrosaque flumina victos —

or a procession of captives,

> Incedunt victae longo ordine gentes,
> Quam variae linguis, habitu tam vestis et armis.[1]
>
> _Æn._ viii. 630 _ff._

JUDGMENT OF EMPEROR.

The whole is a glorification of the Roman empire and a deification of Augustus. Homer's shield was the representation of a general idea, while Virgil's is personal and national. An early work of Pheidias, in celebration of the victory at Marathon, was national, but it was more ideal

---

[1] The long procession of conquered nations goes wending along. Look at the endless variety in their clothes and armour.

than that which Virgil describes, and the figures were probably statues and not reliefs. Athena and Apollo with Miltiades were the three chief statues, these are accompanied by the heroes of Attica—

ἐκ δὲ τῶν ἡρώων καλουμένων Ἐρεχθεύς τε καὶ Κέκροψ καὶ Πανδίων, καὶ Λεώς τε καὶ Ἀντίοχος ὁ ἐκ Μήδας Ἡρακλεῖ γενόμενος τῆς Φύλαντος.—Paus. x. 10, I

—but of course there could be no crowded lines of captives or figures representing conquered countries, such as Virgil introduces under the names of the Nile, Euphrates, and Rhine. Other national Greek monuments, as those of the Tegeans, Argives and others, are mentioned by Pausanias. But these were composed of grouped statues of gods and heroes, and do not appear to have had more than one or two of the principal leaders like Miltiades or Lysander, which could be real representations of historical personages. It is quite true that some of the Greek sculptures, as the Phigalean frieze, the Nereid monument, and that of the temple of Nike Apteros, contain groups which may be called complicated, but they are never confused, as those on the Roman arches are. The nearest approach in Greek monuments to multitudinous confusion is to be found in the moving bodies of men which are given on the Nereid monument. Plates of these are given in the *Mon. dell. Inst.*

vol. x. tav. xi.—xviii. ; and it will be seen that they are not
nearly so monotonous as the masses of men on those bas-
reliefs of the arch of Constantine, which come from Trajan's
buildings, or on other Roman arches. In parts of the
Nereid frieze, the men are indeed all armed alike and
advance in a line, but we do not find the confused crowds
of the Roman arch friezes. Prof. Michaelis has well said
that they are not more disorderly than some of Homer's
famous lines :

ἀμφὶ δ' ἄρ Αἴαντας δοιοὺς ἵσταντο φάλαγγες
καρτεραὶ, ἃς οὔτ' ἄν κεν Ἄρης ὀνόσαιτο μετελθὼν
οὔτε κ' Ἀθηναίη λαοσσόος. οἱ γὰρ ἄριστοι
κριθέντες Τρῶάς τε καὶ Ἕκτορα δῖον ἔμιμνον,
φράξαντες δόρυ δουρί, σάκος σάκεϊ προθελύμνῳ·
*　　*　　*　　*　　*　　*
ἔγχεα δ' ἐπτύσσοντο θρασειάων ἀπὸ χειρῶν
σειόμεν'· οἱ δ' ἰθὺς φρόνεον, μέμασαν δὲ μάχεσθαι.

Il. xiii. 126.

The poet is here picturing the combined phalanx of the
Greeks resisting the onset of the Trojans, and he points out
to us without confusion the different parts at which they
were close together, their shields, spears, and helmets,
noticing the movement and touch of their crests, and
ending with a remark which gives us the fierce expression
of their countenances. The whole might be represented
without disorder or confusion in sculpture.

We have another monument which goes still farther than the Nereid in anticipating Roman military sculpture, that of the friezes found at Gjolbaschi in Lycia, and now deposited at Vienna.[1] In these Lycian friezes paintings of Polygnotus are supposed to have been imitated, such as are mentioned in Pausanias,

Ὑπὲρ δὲ τὴν Κασσοτίδα ἐστὶν οἴκημα γραφὰς ἔχον τῶν Πολυγνώτου, ἀνάθημα μὲν Κνιδίων, καλεῖται δὲ ὑπὸ Δελφῶν Λέσχη, ὅτι ἐνταῦθασυνιόντες τὸ ἀρχαῖον τά τε σπουδαιότερα διελέγοντο καὶ ὁπόσα μυθάδη.—x. 25 ;

and are to be seen on some vases of the end of the fifth century B.C. The prosaic details of Roman arch sculpture are approached in some of these friezes, as they are on the Nereid monument, for we have assaults of city walls, long strings of prisoners, and also scenes of common life, like the loading of beasts of burden by the defeated people who are carrying away their household goods. Pictorial influences also are strongly marked on all these scenes, the execution of which cannot be placed later than the end of the fifth century B.C. But, as we should naturally expect from the far wider and more complicated motives of sculptors under imperial influences, the Lycian friezes are much less crowded and more well proportioned than the Roman. The Lycian representations are grouped, the

---

[1] Perry's *Catalogue*, No. 136.

H

Roman are crowded. Moreover there is one feature in the Lycian friezes which is not reproduced on the Roman, at least to a like extent. Legendary figures form a part of the larger groups in the Greek designs, as in those of Nereids, Amazons, and Centaurs, they do. Now though

BURNING OF ACCOUNT BOOKS.

it is true that gods and legendary heroes are introduced by the later Roman poets and sculptors, yet they occupy a much more secondary part than in Greek poetry or sculpture. In a similar manner battles and military engagements, as well as household affairs, are placed in Greek sculpture much more than in Roman under the direct control and patronage of supernatural and heroic beings. The commencements of the *Iliad* and the *Æneid*, as mentioned above, must have often been noticed and compared by students.   The Muse is invoked and the designs of Zeus are spoken of by Homer, while Virgil trusts to his own powers to tell the story, and only calls in the Muse to state the divine influences which operated upon the intercourse of the various characters.   Immediate action of the gods is much more distinct in the *Iliad* than in the *Æneid*.

A striking instance of the military and imperial tendency of later republican Roman art is to be recognised in the accounts of the famous colonnade of the theatre built by Pompey the Great and called *porticus ad nationes*.   In this colonnade we are told by Pliny of the fourteen nations—

Idem Varro et a Coponio xiv nationes quae sunt circa Pompei theatrum factas auctor est.—*Nat. Hist.* xxxvi. 41.

And Suetonius speaks of Nero's imaginary alarms at the visions of troops :

Modo a simulacris gentium ad Pompei theatrum dedicatarum circumiri arcerique progressu.—*Nero.* xlvi.[1]

---

[1] Now he was surrounded by troops of the nations represented round Pompey's theatre, and was prevented from stirring.

The statue of Germania devicta in the Leggia dei Lanzi at Florence is said [1] to be probably similar to these statues in the colonnade of Pompey's theatre. Such imperial designs were not unknown, though much rarer in Greek art. The Greek representations, as was natural, were generally executed in painting rather than sculpture,[2] and but few early instances of statues erected in praise of military exploits can be mentioned.[3] Those of Harmodius and Aristogeiton are the best known of earlier times. In the Alexandrine epoch and under the influence of Lysippus historical military sculpture became much more frequent. In Rome as in Greece this kind of painting of course preceded sculpture.

Dignatio autem praecipua Romae increvit, ut existimo, a M'. Valerio Maxumo Massala, qui princeps tabulam pictam preli quo Carthaginienses et Hieronem in Sicilia vicerat proposuit in latere curiae Hostiliae anno ab urbe condita ccccxc. Fecit hoc idem et L. Scipio tabulamque victoriae suae Asiaticae in Capitolio posuit, idque aegre tulisse fatrem Africanum tradunt haud immerito, quando filius eius illo proelio captus fuerat. Non dissimilem offensionem et Aemiliani subiit Lucius Hostilius Mancinus qui primus Carthaginem inruperat situm eius oppugnationesque depictas proponendo in foro et ipse adsistens populo spectanti singula enarrando, qua comitate proxumis comitiis

---

[1] Perry, *Greek and Roman Sculpture*, pp. 561, 629.
[2] See Müller, *Hdbk.* § 135.
[3] See Perry, *Gr. Sculp.* p. 636.

consulatum adeptus est. Habuit et scaena ludis Claudi Pulchri mag-
nam admirationem picturae, cum ad tegularum similitudinem corvi
decepti imaginem advolarent.—Plin. *Nat. Hist.* xxxv. 4, 7.

It will be known to all students of Roman coinage how
much the influence of national pride prevailed in that
department of their art. I need only quote the conclud-
ing sentences of that admirable work, *Les Médaillons de
l'Empire Romain*, by W. Frœhner, to shew how perva-
sive this characteristic is. He says, p. 346: ' La monnaie
Romaine est essentiellement patriotique. Le culte des
dieux, les souvenirs du passé, les mérites des princes, et de
leurs familles, les faits de guerre ; voilà son domaine propre,
et dont il ne s'écarte pas. Une fois choisis, les types se main-
tiennent avec ténacité. Tant qu'ils durent, ils conservent
toute leur justesse et leur à-propos. S'ils cèdent la place
à des sujets nouveaux, c'est qu'ils n'ont plus de raison
d'être. J'insiste sur cette grande qualité de la numis-
matique de Rome. Peu d'imagination, beaucoup d'énergie,
et un sentiment profond de la vérité historique. Là est
sa force et son intérêt.'

ESSAY III.

COMPOSITE AND COLOSSAL ART.

WE now proceed from the features immediately produced in Roman art by national characteristics to the modification of those features by external circumstances, such as imperial world-wide sway, exorbitant wealth, and luxurious refinement. These influences complicated and destroyed the early simplicity of Græco-Roman art, and explain why Persius spoke of it as foam and fat:

> *Arma virum*, nonne hoc spumosum et cortice pingui?
> Ut ramale vetus praegrandi subere coctum.—*Sat.* 1. 96.[1]

The Corinthian capital was elaborated into the Composite capital, the forcible and striking hexameter of Ennius and Lucretius was changed from the evenly-flowing well-

---

[1] Arms and the man ! (an ejaculation, comparing the catalogue style of these poets with that of Virgil.) Can one call this anything but froth and clammy bark, like an old dried up branch with a huge knotty bark upon it ?

grouped correctly-finished verses of Virgil to the rhetorical
style of Lucan, flooded with long descriptions, catalogues,
and epigrammatic speeches ; it was changed from Scipio's

TOMB OF SCIPIO.

simple tomb to the mausoleum of Augustus, with its
bronze statues, its massive Babylonian ledged terraces, and
its oriental approach flanked with Egyptian obelisks.   Nor
was it only in the style and subjects of their poetry, or in

TOMB AT ATHENS.

the ornamentation of their monumental designs that this
influence made itself felt. Foreign and oriental mythology
introduced itself and brought a composite mixture of
gods, heroes, personifications, strange modes of worship,
and superstitions innumerable.

The danger to which Roman poetical art was exposed
by the intrusion of foreign and oriental mythology and art,
and a disposition to adopt and combine them with Latin
design and execution, is spoken of by Horace in one of
his best known critical satires :

> Atque ego cum Graecos facerem, natus mare citra,
> Versiculos, vetuit me tali voce Quirinus:
> In silvam non ligna feras insanius ac si
> Magnas Graecorum malis implere catervas !
>
> *Sat.* I. 10, 31.

The attempt to render their style ornate and to look
learned was naturally the chief cause of this mixture of
Greek with Latin, the extent of which will be familiar to
the readers of Lucilius and of most early Latin poets,
and to those who are fond of reading Cicero's letters.
Horace exclaims that to imitate a mere Pitholeon was easy
enough,

> At magnum fecit, quod verbis Graeca Latinis
> Miscuit.   O seri studiorum ! quine putetis

Difficile et mirum, Rhodio quod Pitholeonti
Contigit?—*Sat.* 1, 10, 20.[1]

Pitholeon having mixed Latin and Greek in his epigrammatic verses.   Cicero in his treatise, *Brutus*, ch.
xix. § 75, when comparing the pleasure which may be
derived from contemplating some of the beauties of
poetry with those which art yields, says, speaking of the
older Roman poets and of Nævius in particular,

> Tamen illius (Naevii) quem in vatibus et Faunis numerat Ennius,
> bellum Punicum, quasi Myronis opus, delectat.—*Brutus,* xix. 75 ;

that the pleasure derived from his poetry was like that
derived from Myron's sculpture.   He seems to refer to the
representation of complex groups of warriors for which
Myron is called by Ovid a workman who produced many
laborious works of art :

> Quae nunc nomen habent operosi signa Myronis,
> Pondus iners quondam duraque massa fuit.
> *Ar. Am.* iii. 219.

The fondness of the Romans for composite works of art is
here clearly shewn, for it is not only from a desire to praise

---

[1] But still he did a great thing.   He introduced Greek words into
his Latin.   You're a long way behind the age in your studies if you
think that difficult which a Rhodian like Pitholeon could do.

antique poetry that Cicero is speaking but to express his general admiration of pictorial poetry. The confusion of religious cults and the complex crowd of deities brought before the Romans may be first mentioned.

ARCH OF SEPTIMIUS SEVERUS.

The satirists launch their criticisms on the popular delusions to which a medley of religious insanity led. The multitudinous variety of deities which were adored more or less by the Roman people may be seen by reading the arguments of the Academic philosopher Cotta in the third book of Cicero's treatise, *On the Nature of Gods.* He there enumerates catalogues of beings held divine to the extent of many chapters full of the names of deified heroes, and a list of personified human feelings mental as well as corporeal is detailed. Cotta's purpose was to shew how absurd, when carefully considered, polytheism appeared :

Ergo hoc aut in immensum serpet, aut nihil horum recipiemus, nec illa infinita ratio superstitionis probabitur.—*De N. D.* iii. 52.[1]

Another passage of Cicero's shews the mixture of Greek and oriental divinities at Rome in a way which might be illustrated by thousands of quotations from the Latin writers. He speaks of Serapis, an Egyptian deity, and Æsculapius, the Greek god of healing, as standing on the same footing to the Roman ; and even Cicero thus makes a mixture of Greek and oriental mythology :

An Æsculapius, an Serapis potest nobis praescribere per somnium curationem valetudinis.—*De Div.* ii. 123.

A passage in Tacitus shews this confusion in mythology at Rome. It was disputed whether Serapis was a name for Osiris, Æsculapius, or Jupiter, or Dis ; and the historian

---

[1] So this will creep on till it becomes measureless in extent ; we shall accept none of it, and not approve of that endless superstitious way of going on.

says that the mythological critics differed in opinion, and
had no definite views :

Deum ipsum multi Aesculapium, quod medeatur aegris corporibus,
quidam Osirin, antiquissimum illis gentibus numen, plerique Iovem
ut rerum omnium potentem, plurimi Ditem patrem insignibus quae in
ipso manifesta aut per ambages coniectant.—*Hist.* iv. 84.

A mixture of Greek legend with Latin mythological
personification is perhaps most clearly seen in the *Thebaid*
of Statius, where the goddess of Virtue inspires Menœceus
to sacrifice himself for the good of his country.   He stabs
himself on the walls and sprinkles them with his blood,
and finally is received in Virtue's arms, who only provides
for the gentle descent of his body, but his spirit meantime
ascends into heaven :

Sic ait insignemque animam mucrone corusco
Dedignantem artus pridem moestamque teneri
Arripit, atque uno quaesitam volnere rumpit.
Sanguine tunc spargit turres et moenia lustrat,
Seque super medias acies, nondum ense remisso,
Jecit et in saevos cadere est conatus Achivos.
Ast illum amplexae Pietas Virtusque ferebant
Leniter ad terras corpus, nam spiritus olim
Ante Jovem et summis apicem sibi poscit in astris.

Theb. x. 774.[1]

---

[1] So he speaks, and with one stab he reaches his spirit which had
long been despising his body, and was sad at being kept back, and

The death of Capaneus in the *Thebaid* also illustrates
Roman as compared with Grecian mythology.   Jupiter
even feels respect for that villain as a great warrior and
successful chief, and so far from being punished by the
pains of Tartarus he is received with honour by the whole
region :

> Torvus adhuc visu memorandaque facta relinquens
> Gentibus, atque ipsi non illaudata Tonanti.
>
> *Theb.* xi. 10.
>
> Dum coetu Capaneus laudatur ab omni
> Ditis, et insignem Stygiis fovet amnibus umbram.
>
> *Theb.* xi. 70.

If we look through the titles of the divinities used
by Virgil and Horace we shall find but few which
are exclusively Latin.   The whole structure of their
spiritual and heavenly world is laid out in Greek form,
but the names are changed.   The Camœnæ are iden-
tical with the Musæ, Diana with Artemis, Liber with
Bacchus, Minerva with Athena, and numbers of other
deities have two names at least in the Latin poets.   If

---

sets it free.   Then he sprinkles the towers with blood, and with a look
at the walls, sword in hand, he hurls himself into the centre of the
fighting body, and tries to fall upon the savage Achæans.   But Piety
and Virtue embrace his body tenderly, and carry it gently to the
ground ; long before had his spirit ascended to Jupiter, and was
claiming the topmast place among the highest star

COLISEUM.

we turn to Lucan, the place of Jupiter is taken by
Fortuna :

> Quos undique traxit
> In miseram Fortuna necem, dum munera longi
> Explicat eripiens aevi, populosque ducesque
> Constituit campis : per quos tibi, Roma, ruenti
> Ostendat quam magna cadas.—*Phars.* vii. 415

The modifications made by the Romans in the characters
of these borrowed or assumed deities correspond very
nearly to those which the Romans made in Greek architecture and sculpture. Let us take one of the pairs of
those mentioned above, and we shall find a parallel in the
changes made by the Romans in the Corinthian and Ionic
capitals. Athena was 'full of ideas' in Homer ; and we
find Minerva in Ovid 'called the goddess of thousands of
works.' So in like manner the Corinthian capital is the
ideal of simply beautiful ornament, while the Composite
is rich and complicated. The Greek Ionic is simple, while
the Roman Ionic is architecturally adapted in form.

The Roman's notion of pleasure derived from art was
social happiness and friendly intercourse, promoted by
building wide and decorative public halls with numbers
of statues and other attractive sights, or hearing long
tedious recitations ; while the Greek notion of pleasure
in art was to be able to gaze with adoration on the symmetrical groups of sculptures in and upon his temples,

TEMPLE OF NIKE.

or to hear the noble and lofty odes of Pindar, or the grandly simple choruses of Æschylus and Sophocles.

Hence the introduction of a compound series of gods and heroes was characteristic of the Roman poets, as it was in Roman sculpture and probably in Roman painting. It is often observed by the critics of Virgil that he has built up a compound legend to suit his poem of the *Æneid* by a use of the statements made by the Sicilian authors Stesichorus and Timæus about Æneas, which he has connected with the Latin legend of the *Julia gens* through Julus.

The vulgar display of wide rule is laughed at by the satirists, as by Horace :

> Turgidus Alpinus iugulat dum Memnona dumque
> Defingit Rheni luteum caput.—*Sat.* i. 10, 36.

Cicero says of the dilution of Greek eloquence that it lost the healthy tone and purity by being mixed with Asiatic and overwrought attempts to give fullness without regard for symmetry :

> Nam ut semel e Piraeeo eloquentia evecta est, omnes peragravit insulas, atque ita peregrinata tota Asia est, ut se externis oblineret moribus, omnemque illam salubritatem Atticae dictionis et quasi sanitatem perderet ac loqui paene dedisceret.—*Brutus*, 51.

Propertius felt the power of imperial influence and widely extended national dominion and has expressed

PORTA NIGRA, AT TREVES.

in several poems his wish to celebrate great triumphs
and historical events at length, but says he is deterred
by his feelings of the immense labour it would involve.
He therefore wisely avoids any national epic, and represents Phœbus as checking his ardour in the same way in
which Horace does:

> Quid tibi cum tali, demens, est flumine? quis te
> Carminis heroi tangere jussit opus?
> Non hinc ulla tibi speranda est fama, Properti ;
> Mollia sunt parvis prata terenda rotis.—iv. 2,

The *Sæcular Ode* of Horace is a most complete specimen
of the combination of Roman with general mythology
used by the poet to adorn his deified Augustus, and this
feature of the poem has been admirably stated by Otto
Jahn in his popular essays on ancient art, where he traces
out clearly the connexion between this ode and the famous
prima porta statue of Augustus.   We find the same
mixture of Latin and Greek deities.   We have the
Latin goddess Diana addressed in the ode by the Greek
name Eilithyia and also by her Latin name Lucina,
which belongs also to Juno and Luna.   We have Apollo
addressed as Phœbus, the sun god, and Ceres united
with Tellus.   We have also the Roman tendency to
combination in full force, for Horace guides his hymn of
worship by way of Æneas to the emperor Augustus,

Clarus Anchisae Venerisque sanguis.

Carm. Sæc. 50.

and then breaks out into allusions to the world-wide
sway of the Roman empire :

Iam mari terraque manus potentes
Medus Albanasque timet secures ;
Iam Scythae responsa petunt, superbi
Nuper, et Indi.

Ib. 53.

But he proceeds to say that foreign policy and conquest
are not Rome's only glory. Peace and other personified
high qualities—Fides, Honor, Pudor, Virtus, and Copia
—reign throughout the world, and thus he adorns his
previous combinations.

On the statue of Augustus we have also a conglomeration of symbols and figures. On the upper part of the
breast-plate the god of heaven and the sun-god driving his
chariot, preceded by the deities of sunrise and dew, appear.
Below him are two figures, one of which represents a
Roman general to whom the other is handing over a
Roman standard. This probably represents the recovery
of the standard lost by the Germans, and the final peace
concluded with the Parthians. On each side of these
figures are captives bringing articles which denote the
spoils of war. These may be the Medus, Scythæ, and
Indi of Horace. Below these two figures we have Apollo

riding on a griffin, Diana, and in the lowest place as the
foundation of all Roman wealth, Tellus, with a *cornu
copiæ*. The Oriental power of Rome is represented by an
Egyptian sphinx on each shoulder plate.

If we take one of the principal scenes in the twenty-
second book of the *Iliad* and one from the eighth book
of the *Pharsalia*, where the death of Hector in the former
and of Pompeius in the latter are the central points, we
shall see how complicated and consequently weakened the
surroundings are in Lucan, and how simple and striking in
Homer. In the *Iliad* we have Priam, Hecuba, and
Andromache drawn simply with vivid touches, the short
speeches of each of the three are most striking, without
any distracting accompaniments.

PRIAM.

τῶν πάντων οὐ τόσσον ὀδύρομαι ἀχνύμενός περ
ὡς ἑνός, οὗ μ᾽ ἄχος ὀξὺ κατοίσεται Ἄϊδος εἴσω,
Ἕκτορος· ὡς ὄφελεν θανέειν ἐν χερσὶν ἐμῇσιν.

Il. xxii. 424.

HECUBA.

τέκνον, ἐγὼ δειλὴ τί νυ βείομαι, αἰνὰ παθοῦσα,
σεῦ ἀποτεθνηῶτος; ὅ μοι νύκτας τε κὰι ἦμαρ
εὐχωλὴ κατὰ ἄστυ πελέσκεο, πᾶσί τ᾽ ὄνειαρ,
Τρωσί τε καὶ Τρωῇσι κατὰ πτόλιν, οἵ σε θεὸν ὣς
δειδέχατ᾽· ἦ γαρ κέ σφι μάλα μέγα κῦδος ἔησθα
ζωὸς ἐών· νῦν αὖ θάνατος καὶ Μοῖρα κιχάνει.

Il. xxii. 431.

ANDROMACHE.

Ἕκτορ, ἐγὼ δύστηνος· ἰῇ ἄρα γιγνόμεθ᾽ αἴσῃ
ἀμφότεροι, σὺ μὲν ἐν Τροίῃ Πριάμου κατὰ δῶμα,
αὐτὰρ ἐγὼ Θήβῃσιν ὑπὸ Πλάκῳ ὑληέσσῃ.

Il. xxii. 477.

Lucan, after reciting Cornelia's appeal to the assassins
that they should first kill her, as Pompey would be more
afflicted by her death than his own, distracts our attention
by speaking of the Egyptian embalmment of Pompey's
head,

Tunc arte nefanda
Submota est capiti tabes : raptoque cerebro
Exsiccata cutis, putrisque effluxit ab alto
Humor, et infuso facies solidata veneno est.

viii. 688 ;

then introduces an address to Ptolemy,

Ultima Lageae stirpis, perituraque proles,
Degener, incestae sceptris cessure sororis,
Cum tibi sacrato Macedon servetur in antro,
Et regum cineres exstructo monte quiescant,
Cum Ptolemaeorum manes seriemque pudendam
Pyramides claudant, indignaque Mausolea :
Litora Pompeium feriunt, truncusque vadosis
Huc illuc iactatur aquis.   Adeone molesta
Totum cura fuit socero servare cadaver ?

viii. 693 ;

and then announces the arrival of Cordus, who performs funeral ceremonies at some length, ending in a strange and offensive manner.

In the speeches which Homer puts into the mouth of his characters we have simple affectionate sorrow and recollection of past happiness, while Lucan throughout his account of Pompey's mourners inserts descriptions of the disgusting parts of his murder, and appeals to the feelings of his readers. Thus we lose the higher tone of grief, and come down to disagreeable and unsightly features. The Greek poet is beautiful, the Roman horrid.

The extended and therefore diluted plot of the *Æneid*, as compared with that of the *Iliad*, may be quoted as an instance of the first beginnings of the influence exercised on Roman art by the wide empire of the Romans. In the *Æneid* we have the voyages of Æneas detailed and his visits to various places, at each of which a different scene is added to the picture. It may be said that the travels of Odysseus, as related in the *Odyssey*, are of the same nature. But in the *Odyssey* we have more a legendary tale and a less divided and extended one. By the introduction of Dido and Camilla in the *Æneid* a more decidedly dramatic feature is given to both the former and the latter parts of the story. The prophetic strain

also, to which the visit of Æneas to Hades gives
utterance, carries us over vast regions and into many
places and extends the prospect widely.   In his descriptions of the combats between the Rutulians and Trojans,
Virgil is more apt to stray from the exact point set before
us than Homer is.   For instance, the defeat of Ornytus
by Camilla is enlarged by a divergent description
of the hero's clothing :

> Cui pellis latos humeros erepta iuvenco
> Pugnatori operit ; caput ingens oris hiatus
> Et malae texere lupi cum dentibus albis,
> Agrestisque manum armat sparus.
>
> *Æn.* xi. 679.

The luxury of the Etruscans, which is quite foreign
to the point, intrudes in another passage :

> At non in Venerem segnes nocturnaque bella,
> Aut, ubi curva choros indixit tibia Bacchi,
> Exspectare dapes et plenae pocula mensae ;
> Hic amor, hoc studium, dum sacra secundus haruspex
> Nuntiet, ac lucos vocet hostia pinguis in altos.
>
> *Æn.* xi. 736.

Again, an instance of additional foreign matters used
as extraneous ornament may be seen in the tenth
book :

Namque ferunt luctu Cycnum Phaethontis amati,
Populeas inter frondes umbramque sororum
Dum canit et moestum Musa solatur amorem,
Canentem molli pluma duxisse senectam,
Linquentem terras et sidera voce sequentem.
Filius, aequales comitatus classe catervas,
Ingentem remis Centaurum promovet: ille
Instat aquae saxumque undis inmane minatur
Arduus, et longa sulcat maria alta carina.

Æn. x. 189.

The poet's antiquarian love of old mythological legend
leads him astray and induces him to waste his powers and
confuse his readers by unnecessary reference to the love of
Phaethon and metamorphosis of Cycnus.

In the *Iliad*, on the other hand, the poet seldom strays
beyond the plains of Troy or the Greek mainland and
Ionian islands. The greater part of the fighting in the
twelfth and thirteenth books is carried on at the defences
raised by the Greeks to protect their ships. This is the
furthest position to which the engagements move.
Throughout these books the fighting is carried on by
individual heroes, or in duels between pairs of heroes,
seldom by any rush or move of an armed body of
them.

Above the whole, we have the celestial group of gods
exercising a control, and interfering occasionally. We are
reminded of their influence by the poet in such passages

as the announcement of dependence on their will at the
beginning of the twelfth book—

$$\theta\epsilon\tilde{\omega}\nu\ \delta'\ \grave{a}\acute{\epsilon}\kappa\eta\tau\iota\ \tau\acute{\epsilon}\tau\nu\kappa\tau o$$
$$\grave{a}\theta a\nu\acute{a}\tau\omega\nu\cdot\ \tau\grave{o}\ \kappa a\grave{\iota}\ o\breve{\upsilon}\tau\iota\ \pi o\lambda\upsilon\nu\chi\rho\acute{o}\nu o\nu\ \breve{\epsilon}\mu\pi\epsilon\delta o\nu\ \mathring{\eta}\epsilon\nu.$$

Il. xii. 8.

It is true that the gods interfere in the course of events
in the *Æneid*, but the great council of Olympus is not ever
present to the mind, seated above in the heavens, and
lying " beside their nectar."

In the later Roman epic poets the composite nature of
their art becomes much more visible than in Virgil. Virgil,
as we have seen, introduces foreign allusions now and then,
without distracting the mind seriously, and uses the prophetic and historic tone in digressions only with a distinct
purpose, and keeps up throughout reference to a higher
power of control, similar to, though not so strong as, that
of Homer. But when we examine the *Pharsalia* of Lucan
we are confused by the variety of the chords he keeps
striking, and we cannot always recognise the prominent
chord which ought to pervade the whole of his work.
Lucan's purpose evidently is that of ostentatiously
parading the vast extent of the philosophical, geogra-
phical, and ethnological knowledge which was almost
forced upon his mind by the vast imperial dominions

CROWD ON SARCOPHAGUS.

of Rome. The note which we find dominating is the irresistible power of Rome. But this is expressed in a lumbering and overwhelming manner, and not by fine touches, as the key-note is in Homer and Virgil.

No one can deny the genius of Lucan, but the whole effect of his poem is not great, on account of the distractions caused by its composite nature. This fault is mainly produced by the circumstances under which he lived. Virgil had begun to feel the deteriorating influences of the empire, but they are only shewn slightly in his poetry as compared with that of Lucan. Let us trace out some of these ponderous catalogue-like enumerations.

In the first book of the *Pharsalia* we have a list of prodigies given at length, extending through fifty-six lines in a dull and uninteresting manner.

In the second book a detailed account of the ferocious party quarrels in Rome, extending through hundreds of lines.

In the third book there is a long dull description of the siege of Marseilles, and similar merely enumerative descriptions may be read in each of the following books.

Commenting on the Roman sarcophagus in the Vatican

museum, which represents a battle of gods and giants, a writer in the *Journal of Hellenic Studies*, vol. iii. p. 329, alluding to the Pergamene frieze, and comparing it with the sarcophagus, says, " In this last quoted Roman work there is this other similarity and this point of difference as compared with the Pergamene : a general gigantomachy is rendered, and no scenes of separate conflicts, but the giants are so banded together as actors in a common cause that individual interest is lacking." Illustrations of the difference here mentioned between Roman and Greek art may be taken from natural scenery and growth. Who does not see more exquisite and varied beauty in the aspect of a simple tree standing by itself, or in a group of trees, than in a monotonous row of trees, all of which are growing in the exact places, and to the exact height of each other ? Or take another example of the same kind. Is there not more various and elegant beauty in a plant of corn, or of fern, or of prairie grass, than in a field of corn, or a number of plants set in order and arranged in lines, to suit the square shape of a field or garden ? Is not a garden more beautiful when planted in groups or in an irregular manner, than when formally arranged and crowded ?

Thus we find, as is natural in the later poets compared with those of the Augustan age, many more examples of the special influence which the wide dominion and complicated system of the Roman Empire had upon their minds.   Each poet desirous of decorating his work has taken the same points of interest.   But in the one class we have a few striking examples, combined harmoniously, while in the other we have a long, tedious, dull and monotonous reiteration.

Thus we have in the first book of the *Pharsalia* the long list of prodigies quoted above extending over fifty-seven lines.   But in the first book of the *Georgics* these are contracted and made much more forcible in the well-known passage beginning at line 466 and ending after twenty-three splendid lines.   In the same way that melancholy catalogue of horrors in the seventh book of the *Pharsalia* may be contrasted with the carefully selected scenes in the second and third books of the *Æneid*, and the concise phrases at the end of the first book of the *Georgics*.

> Huic movet Euphrates, illinc Germania bellum,
> Vicinae ruptis inter se legibus urbes
> Arma ferunt ; saevit toto Mars impius orbe.
>
> *Georg.* i 509.

To take another department of Epic poetry.   In Homer's description of battles we have the valour of one hero illustrated or a duel fought between two, while

in Lucan we have the advance of trained bodies of troops
or of masses of men.

> Densis acies stipata catervis.
> > *Phars.* vii. 492.
> Per populos hic Roma perit.
> > Id. vii. 634.

The forces of Pompey are described at unnecessary
length and with almost the dullness of an army list in
Phars. iii. 169—284, while in the enumeration of the Greek
and Trojan armies in *Il.* ii. Homer lights up his list with
sparkling vigour here and there, and entirely prevents the
feeling of monotony. Virgil, too, is very successful in his
interesting accounts of the allies of Æneas and Turnus in
the seventh and eleventh books of the *Æneid.* The defect
in poetic art here is the same as we have before noticed in
sculpture, when we compared the hosts crowded on the
reliefs of the triumphal arches and the sarcophagi, with the
symmetrical groups of the Parthenon, and in a less degree
with those of the Nereid monument.

The influence of their vast empire on the minds of the
Romans may be traced not only by the composite nature
of their literature and art, but in its bulk and ponderous
mass. Pliny and Juvenal have pointed this out in concise
sayings. In his *Natural History*, xxxiv. 39, Pliny speaks
of colossal statues and great collections of works of art as
instances of rash boldness :

Audaciae innumera sunt exempla.—Plin. *Nat. Hist.* xxxiv. VII. 18.
Adeo materiam conspici malunt omnes quam se nosci.—Id. xxxv. II. 2.[1]

And Juvenal also has a line expressing a well-known effect of wide wealth upon taste :

Magis illa iuvant quae pluris emuntur.—*Sat.* xi. 16.

Colossal figures and vast collections of art were paralleled in literature by the encyclopædic and voluminous writings of jurists and historians and poets.   These are satirised by Juvenal,

> Namque oblita modi millesima pagina surgit
> Omnibus, et multa crescit damnosa papyro.
> Sic ingens rerum numerus iubet atque operum lex.[2]
> > *Sat.* vii. 100.

Dion Cassius, lxii. 29, says of the jurist Cornatus that he was banished by Nero because he had recommended the emperor not to write four hundred books in his poem on Troy, a performance which the parasites had said would be applauded by the Roman public.

---

[1] So anxious are they that vast construction should be surveyed with wonder, rather than that they should themselves be seen.

[2] For without any method they all write thousands of pages, and fill column after column of papyrus.

K

Martial's remark upon Livy's history is that his library is too small to hold all of it.

Quem mea non totum bibliotheca capit.[1]—*Ep.* xiv. 186.

The encyclopædic character of later Roman literature and art is too well known to need many illustrations, but we may point out some of the early instances. A comparison of Virgil's description of Ætna with that of Pindar has been a familiar subject of discussion among critics from the time of Gellius, who gives the opinion of Favorinus in the reign of Hadrian preferring Pindar.

In Pindar we have a few simple masterly strokes. Fountains of fire are belched forth. Then first a cloud of smoke rises by day from the rivers of molten lava, and secondly, by night the volcano flings rocks upward which fall with a crash in the sea.

τᾶς ἐρεύγονται μὲν ἀπλάτου πυρὸς ἁγνόταται
ἐκ μυχῶν παγαί· ποταμοὶ δ' ἁμέραισιν μὲν προχέοντι ῥόον καπνοῦ
αἴθων'· ἀλλ' ἐν ὄρφναισιν πέτρας
φοίνισσα κυλινδομένα φλὸξ ἐς βαθεῖαν φέρει πόντου πλάκα σὺν πατάγῳ.

Pyth. i. 21.

But Virgil overpaints the scene and gives a crowded description :

---

[1] Why, my whole library would not hold his works.

Horrificis iuxta tonat Aetna ruinis
Interdumque atram prorumpit ad aethera nubem,
Turbine fumantem piceo et candente favilla,
Attollitque globos flammarum et sidera lambit ;
Interdum scopulos avolsaque viscera montis
Erigit eructans, liquefactaque saxa sub auras
Cum gemitu glomerat, fundoque exaestuat imo.

Æn. iii. 57.

Favonius justly remarked against Virgil on the above lines
that they are too wordy and elongated :

Virgilius dum in strepitu sonituque verborum conquirendo
laborat, utrumque tempus noctis et diei nulla discretione facta,
confudit.—Gellius, xvii. 10.

The tendency of the Roman poets and artists upon
which we are now dwelling is shewn in Virgil's high-
sounding words, and the complication of his smoke and
flame and discharges of ashes and fragments, while we
have a clear representation in Pindar of fire, smoke, lava,
and volleys of stones thrown up.

The addition of ornament, unnecessary display, and
complicated design of which we have spoken is produced,
partly by the world-wide extension of Roman thought and
partly by the fancies of rich patronage. It may be illustrated by comparing Homer's description of the eagle
appearing as an omen to the armies when about to attack

K 2

with the same scene in Virgil. In *Iliad* xii. 200, we have
eight masterly lines :

> ὄρνις γὰρ σφιν ἐπῆλθε, περησέμεναι μεμαῶσιν,
> αἰετὸς ὑψιπέτης, ἐπ᾽ ἀριστερὰ λαὸν ἐέργων,
> φοινήεντα δράκοντα φέρων ὀνύχεσσι πέλωρον,
> ζωὸν ἔτ᾽ ἀσπαίροντα· καὶ οὔπω λήθετο χάρμης.
> κόψε γὰρ αὐτὸν ἔχοντα κατὰ στῆθος παρὰ δειρήν,
> ἰδνωθεὶς ὀπίσω· ὁ δ᾽ ἀπὸ ἕθεν ἧκε χαμᾶζε,
> ἀλγήσας ὀδύνῃσι, μέσῳ δ᾽ ἐνὶ κάββαλ᾽ ὁμίλῳ·
> αὐτὸς δὲ κλάγξας πέτετο πνοιῇς ἀνέμοιο.

and in Virgil, ten :

> Namque volans rubra fulvus Iovis ales in aethra
> Litoreas agitabat aves turbamque sonantem
> Agminis aligeri : subito cum lapsus ad undas
> Cycnum excellentem pedibus rapit improbus uncis.
> Arrexere animos Itali, cunctaeque volucres
> Convertunt clamore fugam, mirabile visu,
> Aetheraque obscurant pennis, hostemque per auras
> Facta nube premunt, donec vi victus et ipso
> Pondere defecit, praedamque ex unguibus ales
> Proiecit fluvio, penitusque in nubila fugit.
>
> *Æn.* xii. 247.

In Virgil the simile assumes a more complicated form
than in Homer. The eagle in Homer is forced by the
snake he has seized whose backward twist is poetically
described in two words, to drop his prey and fly away
down the wind.

But Virgil brings in a host of birds and fills the air with them, and describes their evolutions so as to draw attention to the power of a numerous body of assailants over the eagle, who is not defeated by them alone but also by the overweight of his victim, the swan which he has seized. Homer makes the scene simply striking by a few lines. The snake is whirled up aloft, and deals one deadly bite, while Virgil fills the air with screaming birds who pursue the eagle till he is tired. Other little touches are also added to the picture, the sky is red, the birds are seabirds, the swan is thrown into the river, which are not so apposite as those of Homer.

But it was natural that the imperial influences which, as we have seen, acted strongly upon Roman literature and sculpture, should exert themselves even more strongly upon their architecture. Instances of this will of course occur to every one who has visited Rome, or who has seen the wonderful display of Roman power at Verona, at El Djemm in Tunis, at Pola in Istria, or at Baalbec in Syria. These stupendous monuments of power will at once impress their history vividly upon the mind ; but perhaps it may be suggestive if we turn aside for a moment to remark upon the vast aqueducts which span the Campagna round Rome. It is often asked why the Romans spent so much wealth and labour in erecting these vast ranges of

arches, when they knew perfectly well how to conduct
water in pipes, and did so within the walls of their metropolis to a considerable extent.   An answer to this question
will be found directly when we see it at the point of view

AMPHITHEATRE AT VERONA.

from which we are now considering Roman art.   When
viewed in this light we shall be inclined to take what may
be called "a political view" of the construction of the

aqueducts, as intended mainly to display imperial power, and to give employment to vast numbers of architects and workmen.

A vulgar attempt to display their wealth may also be traced in Roman medallions. Alexander Severus is said to have diminished the extravagant size of the medals which Heliogabalus had made, because he thought that

TEPULAN AND CLAUDIAN AQUEDUCTS.

if the number of coins given was to represent the amount of imperial presents, an equal number of smaller coins would have the same value as one huge medallion.[1] Some of the medallions of the later Empire at the beginning of the fourth century are enormous in size.[2] The emperor

---

[1] Lampréd, *Al. Sev.* 39.   [2] Frœhner, p. 303.

felt that it was a sign of his grandeur and wealth to present these huge masses of precious metal to high officials or to foreign sovereigns.

Many medallions are struck in two metals to display the powers of the mint; and others are decorated with ingeniously curious kinds of dots or patterns, in order to shew to what a vast extent technical skill was encouraged.

Thus in the preceding pages we see how the early Roman epic in Nævius, Ennius and others, had been mainly national, whilst Virgil intermixed another element, that of mythology. Again, in the silver age these two aspects are separated. Lucan and Silius choose national subjects, the Pharsalia and the Punic wars, whilst Statius and Valerius Flaccus go back to the Argonauts and the Thebaica. Yet in each of these poets the same faults appear as in imperial Roman sculpture, shewing how the national mind was affected by empire. To take Statius. After the poet has really told his tale and exhausted his story, we have the imperial composite fashion adopted, and a twelfth book is added containing a long sequel, in which Creon's tyranny, the sorrows of the Argive widows, and the conquest of Thebes by Theseus are expatiated upon. The *Thebaid* of Statius has been well described by the late Professor Conington as "a medley of confused and exaggerated effects, crowding disproportioned incidents and overdrawn or underdrawn characters within the framework of a story which may be a striking one, but which he did not invent but borrow."[1]

A want of simplicity and definite attraction to one point at a time renders the composite faults of Statius very troublesome, as though his reader were intended to hurry on from one incident to another of different character, and as though his object were to draw out a long string of unconnected facts. Thus at the beginning of the *Thebaid* we have the Aonian arms, the sceptre fatal to two kings, the insatiable furies, the funeral flames, the royal deaths, and the brutal carnage in city after city, following each other in an unconnected catalogue. Whether the horrible or the impious, or the extraordinary is to be most impressed on us we have no means of learning, and we rise from the perusal of Statius's poetry with a confused feeling of his cleverness in locking up so many thoughts in an epigrammatic host. From this point of view Conington says of Statius :[2]

"Mr. Merivale has observed with much justice that Statius is a miniature painter employed by the caprice of a patron or his own unadvised ambition on a great historical picture.

---

[1] Conington, *Miscellaneous Writings*, vol. i., p. 370.
[2] *Ibid.* p. 383.

Such exaggerations as his are indeed the fruit of weakness quite as often as of ill-regulated strength. The common-place aspects of a monstrous story may be seized by any quick apprehension, and reproduced by any fertile fancy: it is only high genius that can render them human and credible. Dryden compares Statius to his own Capaneus engaging the two immortals Virgil and Homer, and reaping the fruit of his daring. (Discourse on Epic Poetry prefixed to Dryden's translation of the *Æneid.*) We would rather compare him to his own Atys, the plighted husband of Ismene, who is slain by the mighty arm of Tydeus. The love of his Theban bride leads him into war ; he challenges the champion of the field and falls at the first shock ; and he lies in death pale and bloody, yet in the pride of youthful beauty and golden armour."

ESSAY IV.

TECHNICAL FINISH AND LUXURIOUS REFINEMENT.

SENECA criticises severely the fondness for easily flowing sparkling literature which prevailed in his time among the Romans, and declares that it results from the self-indulgence and luxury of the times, and that genuine strength and vigour of language is sacrificed when a writer uses a brilliant phrase over and over again simply to please the ear of his readers or his audience, and to make his style attractive, not to express deep and solid thought. He compares the style of some writers to the process of shaving and pulling out all the hair which the Romans adopted. The luxurious people he means err, because they like to have their feelings sometimes harrowed and tossed about, which is done by making literature exciting and strange, sometimes by being smoothed and softened, which latter is the common error both in literature and sculpture.

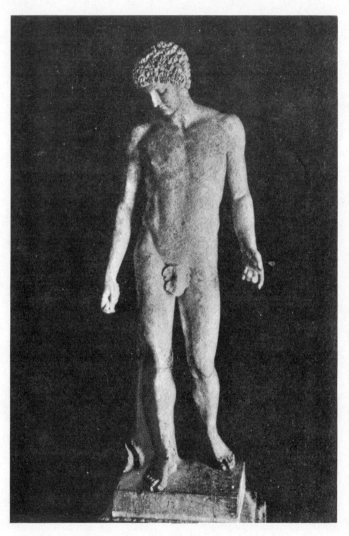

ANTINOUS.

Ad compositionem transeamus : quot genera tibi in hac dabo, quibus peccetur? Quidam praefractam et asperam probant, disturbant de industria, si quid placidius effluxit. Nolunt sine salebra esse iuncturam, virilem putant et fortem, quae aurem inaequalitate percutiat. Quorundam non est compositio, modulatio est : adeo blanditur et molliter labitur.[1]—*Ep.* 114. 15.

Quot vides istos sequi, qui aut vellunt barbam aut intervellunt, qui labra pressius tondent et abradunt servata et submissa cetera parte, qui lacernas coloris inprobi sumunt, qui perlucentem togam, qui nolunt facere quicquam, quod hominum oculis transire liceat? inritant illos et in se advertunt, volunt vel reprehendi, dum conspici : talis est oratio Maecenatis omniumque aliorum, qui non casu errant sed scientes volentesque.[2]—*Ibid.* 21.

Persius attacks this fault of imperial Roman literature which smoothed away all roughness in his first Satire. He represents the author as defending himself by the statement that symmetry is thus maintained, and verse is prevented from taking a harsh and new style.

Sed numeris decor est et iunctura addita crudis.—*Sat.* I. 92.

Persius answers him in the lines which express his

---

[1] In some writers you cannot call it composition, it is modulation, so softly and smoothly does it glide along.

[2] They (who play these absurd tricks with their dress) wish to be looked at even if they are criticised, such is the form of speech used by Maecenas and all others whose mistakes are not made in error, but with full knowledge, and because they wish it.

distrust of such a mode of writing. I hate the lines you call pretty and neat, he says, there is nothing in them.

> Sed recti finemque extremumque esse recuso
> 'Euge' tuum et 'belle'—nam 'belle' hoc excute totum,
> Quid non intus habet? non hic est Ilias Atti
> Ebria veratro non si qua elegidia crudi
> Dictarunt proceres.—*Sat.* i. 48.

The public taste, says the satirist, is wrong in demanding as it does smooth easily running lines, so jointed that the nail of the connoisseur runs easily along.

> Quis populi sermo est? quis enim, nisi carmina molli
> Nunc demum numero fluere, ut per leve severos
> Effundat iunctura unguis? scit tendere versum
> Non secus ac si oculo rubricam derigat uno.[1]—*Sat.* i. 63.

Every student of Latin literature and art will at once recognise many passages and sculptures to which this criticism applies. For instance, in the verses of Ovid elisions are always smoother than in those of Propertius or Catullus. Ovid seldom admits the elision of a long or

---

[1] What does the public say? What, indeed, but that now we at last have verses which flow in smooth measure, so that the critical nail runs evenly along even where the parts join. He can make a line just as if he were ruling it by a cord with one eye shut.

doubtful syllable, except where it almost escapes notice. This sacrifice of forcible thought and expression in some of the Augustan poets and their fondness for superficial and easily intelligible though flat ideas and phrases can be often recognised.

Much of the elegiac poetry of the Romans shews very plainly a love of the exquisite and smooth, as Persius calls it, a technical refinement in the even flow of their verses, and the faultless rhythm of their metre.   Many passages both in elegiac and lyric metres are well known and celebrated for their finish and regularity.   What can be more perfectly level and free from any weakness both in metre and thought than Ovid's tame story about the ride of Tarquin and his friends to find Lucretia in the second book of the *Fasti?*

> Surgit cui dederat clarum Collatia nomen ;
>   Non opus est verbis, credite rebus ait.
> Nox superest : tollamur equis, urbemque petamus.
>   Dicta placent ; frenis impediuntur equi ;
> Pertulerant dominos ; regalia protinus illi
>   Tecta petunt ; custos in fore nullus erat.—*Fasti*, ii. 733.

It flows on like an unruffled stream.   The whole description is without flaw ; but there is no part of it which does not seem more like exquisite needlework than

HERCULES (BRONZE).

powerful design ; a tale told in smooth, elegant verse, rather than a striking and vigorous scene. The thought expressed is common, and the action disagreeable and immoral.

It is more like the Theocritean harmony of song than the solemn organ tones and striking movements in Homer or Virgil. Compare with Ovid's picture that of Ulysses and Diomede starting for their reconnaisance :

> Τὼ δ' ἐπεὶ οὖν ὅπλοισιν ἔνι δεινοῖσιν ἐδύτην,
> βάν ῥ' ἴεναι, λιπέτην δὲ κατ' αὐτόθι πάντας ἀρίστους.
> Τοῖσι δὲ δεξιὸν ἧκεν ἐρωδιὸν ἐγγὺς ὁδοῖο
> Παλλὰς 'Αθηναίη· τοὶ δ' οὐκ ἴδον ὀφθαλμοῖσιν
> νύκτα δι' ὀρφναίην, ἀλλὰ κλάγξαντος ἄκουσαν.
> χαῖρε δὲ τῷ ὄρνιθ' 'Οδυσεὺς, ἠρᾶτο δ' 'Αθήνη
>   *   *   *   *   *
> ὣς ἔφαν εὐχόμενοι· τῶν δ' ἔκλυε Παλλὰς 'Αθήνη
> οἱ δ' ἐπεὶ ἠρήσαντο Διὸς κούρῃ μεγάλοιο,
> βάν ῥ' ἴμεν, ὥστε λέοντε δύω, διὰ νύκτα μέλαιναν,
> ἂμ φόνον, ἂν νέκυας, διά τ' ἔντεα καὶ μέλαν αἷμα.

Il. x. 272.

The fine lines and exquisite detail of the Farnese Hercules or the Apollo Sauroctonos, when compared with the large surfaces and grandeur of the works of Phidias in the Parthenon sculptures, shew the same want of great thought and monumental execution.

Roman art intensified the realism which had appeared in an incipient form in the works of some of the great later

L

Greek sculptors. Lysippus undoubtedly imitated the human form in a closer manner than Phidias or Polycleitus or even Praxiteles, but the Græco-Roman sculptors, under the strong influences of the imperial city, carried imitation so far that they completely separated it from any idealism of the beautiful, and did not stop till in many instances they produced what may be styled caricature.

Sir J. Reynolds says of the picturesque in sculpture :—

" Sculpture is formal, regular, and austere ; disdains all familiar objects, as incompatible with its dignity ; and is an enemy to every species of affectation, or appearance of academical art. All contrast therefore of one figure with another, or of the limbs of a single figure, or even in the folds of the drapery must be sparingly employed. In short, whatever partakes of fancy or caprice, or goes under the denomination of Picturesque, however to be admired in the proper place, is incompatible with that sobriety and gravity which is peculiarly the characteristic of this art." (Sir J. Reynolds, Discourse x. p. 188. Gosse's edition. 1887.)

And again :—

" Upon the whole it seems to me that the object and intention of all the arts is to supply the natural imperfections of things, and often to gratify the mind by realising and embodying what never existed but in the imagination." (Sir J. Reynolds, Discourse xiii. p. 247.)

POMONA.

"The excellence of every art must consist in the complete accomplishment of its purpose, and if by a false imitation of nature, or mean ambition of producing a picturesque effect or illusion of any kind, all the grandeur of ideas which this art endeavours to excite, be degraded or destroyed, we may boldly oppose ourselves to any such innovation. If the producing of a deception be the summit of this art, let us at once give up to statues the addition of colour, which will contribute more towards accomplishing this fact than all the artifices which have been introduced and probably defended, on no other principle but that of rendering the work more natural. But as colour is universally rejected, every practice liable to the same objection must fall with it." (*Deception in Art.* Sir J. Reynolds. Discourse x. p. 175.)

Sir Joshua is wrong here about colour, which was slightly used by the great Greek sculptors.

On the difficulty of producing a general effect in art, Sir J. Reynolds says:—

"A steady attention to the general effect takes up more time and is much more laborious to the mind, than any mode of high finishing or smoothness without such attention."

Mr. Parker says:—

"To the Roman invaders the splendid display of Greek

art—the temples, the poems, and plays, the pictures and statues,—was a novel and interesting phenomenon which captivated the attention and suggested the notion of art for art's sake " (not for the suggestion of any ideas except that of skill). " The Roman did not trouble himself to ask whether the victor in the games had or had not won his prize fairly, or whether the god whose image was carried away would or would not be angered. Pausanias comforts himself with thinking that the disease of which Sulla died was a sign of divine vengeance, but Roman scepticism was proof against such superstition. To the Roman a Greek statue was a statue, and it was nothing more." [1]

" It has been repeatedly said that Homer has genius and Virgil skill, and the proof which is adduced is that the latter does not permit the reader to forget him, while Homer the author is forgotten when the reader takes up the *Iliad*." [2]

The sacrifice of grand motive idea to admiration of technical skill is exemplified in the Laocoon and in other works in which the main motive idea is pain or muscular strength. [3]

---

[1] Parker's *Nature of the Fine Arts*, p. 28.   [2] *Ibid.* p. 346 —28.
[3] See Murray, vol. ii. p. 369.

The latter of these two motives will at once remind the student of some of the figures which are to be seen in any good collection of casts of ancient sculpture. The first of these is the Farnese Hercules, as before said, in which every muscle is brought forward too prominently and is of colossal size to shew the maker's great knowledge of human anatomy, and his perfect skill in representing it most impressively.

Just as Ovid displays his clever art of stringing words together in correct metres, so do the makers of the Laocoon and of the Farnese bull and the Hercules attract attention and applause by their clever modes of grouping, and their minute knowledge of the way in which the muscles expand or contract under extreme tension.

So Tibullus puts the most exquisite finish on his verses, but the subject matter is trivial and ordinary in its tone. He is not equal even to Ovid in his thoughts, but in his poetical style approaches him. The versification of some of his short poems is almost perfect, but the ideas are common. He does this in the following poem :—

> Dicamus bona verba : venit Natalis ad aras ;
>   Quisquis ades lingua, vir mulierque, fave.
> Urantur pia tura focis, urantur odores,
>   Quos tener e terra divite mittit Arabs.

THE WRESTLERS.

Ipse suos Genius adsit visurus honores,
  Cui decorent sanctas mollia serta comas.
Illius puro destillent tempora nardo,
  Atque satur libo sit madeatque mero,
Annuat et, Cornute, tibi, quodcunque rogabis.
  En age, quid cessas? annuit ille : roga.
Auguror, uxoris fidos optabis amores ;
  Iam reor hoc ipsos edidicisse deos.
Nec tibi malueris, totum quaecunque per orbem
  Fortis arat valido rusticus arva bove,
Nec tibi, gemmarum quicquid felicibus Indis
  Nascitur, Eoi qua maris unda rubet.
Vota cadunt, utinam strepitantibus advolet alis
  Flavaque coniugio vincula portet Amor,
Vincula, quae maneant semper, dum tarda senectus
  Inducat rugas inficiatque comas.
Hic veniat Natalis avis prolemque ministret,
  Ludat et ante tuos turba novella pedes.—Tib. ii. 2

A comparison of the neat and compact verse of Ovid with that of Propertius will shew the difference between the technical finish of the Roman court poet and the more rugged and natural expression of one who had partly shaken off the wish to please by elegance and had thoughts which found no rest except in utterance.

The Sapphic odes of Horace give us the most palpable illustration of this technical finish in the outward clothing of thought by poetry. In most of the Sapphic odes the

A DANCING GIRL.

metre is strictly defined and a rigid cæsura is maintained, which makes the lines monotonous. This stiff and formal movement was partly due to the strictness of the Roman character, and partly may have been a result of the national fondness for strict law, and the peculiar aptitude for accurate legal definition which was one of the most remarkable features in the Roman mind, finally developed by Justinian in his *Digest*.

The thoughts in Roman poetry are too much confined by the metre, just as in sculpture the ideas suggested are small and affect details rather than whole figures.

Some of the results of this strong technical spirit, as encouraged by patronage and a desire to save the trouble of thought by accurately adopting fixed rule, are to be seen in Statius. Thus in the *Thebaid* he introduces a book of games as a constituent part of an epic, and does not endeavour to shew that such an interlude is at all appropriate to the action of the poem. In the twenty-sixth book of the *Iliad* and the fifth of the *Æneid* the funeral games have a definite and worthy object, to celebrate the memory of Patroclus and of Anchises, two of the great figures in the poem, but in the *Thebaid* all this display was without meaning, as the poet only deifies an infant in order to justify his interlude, and evidently inserts the book of games only because he thought that his poem would not be complete without such an interlude.

In order to shew what I meant by saying that Propertius had partly shaken off the fashionable primness of the court poet, I will quote two of his poems. In the first we have the strict rules of metre followed by the Ovidian school broken, and simple unaffected thought expressed simply and naturally. In the second we feel the court influence. The language becomes rather more technical :

> Tu qui consortem properas evadere casum
> > Miles, ab Etruscis saucius aggeribus
> Qui nostro gemitu turgentia lumina torques,
> > Pars ego sum vestrae proxima militiae.
> Sic te servato, ut possint gaudere parentes,
> > Nec soror acta tuis sentiat e lacrimis :
> Gallum per medios ereptum Caesaris enses
> > Effugere ignotas non potuisse manus,
> Et quaecunque super dispersa invenerit ossa
> > Montibus Etruscis, haec sciat esse mea.—i. 21.

> Clausus ab umbroso qua ludit Pontus Averno
> > Fumida Baiarum stagna tepentis aquae,
> Qua iacet et Troiae tubicen Misenus arena
> > Et sonat Herculeo structa labore via,
> Hic, ubi, mortales dextra cum quaereret urbes,
> > Cymbala Thebano concrepuere deo,—
> At nunc, invisae magno cum crimine Baiae,
> > Quis deus in vestra constitit hostis aqua ?—

His pressus Stygias vultum demisit in undas,
Errat et in vestro spiritus ille lacu.
Quid genus, aut virtus?—Propertius, iv. 18.

We can plainly see that although the great poets of
Rome, Lucretius, Catullus, Virgil, and Horace, avoided
monotony of rhythm and endeavoured to make their verse
expressive and various, yet in every one of them this
admiration of skill, strengthened by the influence of
luxurious patronage, hampered more or less their efforts
of natural and forcible expression. Virgil and Ovid seem
to apologise for and seek to excuse their abnormal
rhythms, by making use of such rhythms under the
excuse of Greek words and names. Thus we have the
words hyacinthus, hymenæus, melicerta, ambrosius, and
many others of similar kind used to excuse a break in
regularity of metre. The easy versification of the great
Roman poets is marvellous, but becomes somewhat weari-
some and monotonous, whereas the varied tones of
Pindar, or the beautiful changes and forcible outbursts of
Homer or Sophocles, impress the mind with harmonious
majesty. Seneca, in his review of Roman style, quoted
above, says that it cannot be called composition, for
it is really measurement, so softly and smoothly does it
move along.

Perhaps it must be said that Catullus is an exception to

this Roman rule of technical and metrical correctness. When we look at his lyrics we find the Sapphic metre treated with great freedom, the beautiful hendecasyllabic verse sparkling with fanciful ideas, and in his hexameters and elegiacs all the rules observed by Virgil and Ovid are set aside, as he finds that he can make his thoughts more expressive by a turn in the metre. Such lines as some in the noble fragment on the marriage of Peleus and Thetis :

Euhoe bacchantes, euhoe capita inflectentes.—Catull. 64. 256.

Post vento crescente magis magis increbrescunt.—274.

Quo tunc et tellus atque horrida contremuere.
Aequora.—205 ;

or in the lines addressed to his dead brother, where the metre echoes his sobs :

Atque in perpetuum, frater, ave atque vale.
Carm. 101. 10.

are very striking. Catullus does not seek to excuse himself by using Greek words. The picture Catullus draws of Attis (*Carm.* lxiii.) is also one which is less cramped and bound down by the metre than any other piece of Latin poetry. In freedom and expressive point some of the lines are equal to some of the grand Pindaric outbursts :

> Ibi maria vasta visens lacrimantibus oculis,
> Patriam allocuta maesta est ita voce miseriter.
> Ubinam aut quibus locis te positam, patria, reor.
>
> *Carm.* lxiii. 48, 49, 55.

An extract from the writings of a scholar who studied Roman literature very completely may here be given to shew the similarity between Roman and English literature. Professor Conington in his Essay on Pope, says, " Perhaps there is no better help towards a true appreciation of the English poetry of the eighteenth century than a knowledge of the poetry of Augustan Rome. The similarity of the two periods as phases of national literature has often been pointed out ; it would be easy, if this were the place, to pursue the parallel into detail. Now it is curious that what Walsh said to Pope is precisely the same as what Horace said to his countrymen, when he urged correctness of style upon them. Walsh tells them almost in so many words that, though they had several great poets, they never had any one great poet who was correct." And again Conington says, " The ideal which Horace so well described, his ideal poet, was most regular and yet pictorial :

Luxuriantia compescet, nimis aspera sano
Levabit cultu, virtute carentia tollet :
Ludentis speciem dabit et torquebitur ut qui
Nunc Satyrum, nunc agrestem Cyclopa movetur.[1]

Ep. ii. 2. 122.

This was the service which the great writers of the Augustan age rendered to the poetry of their country. If we cannot give them the praise which was bestowed on their Emperor, that where they found brick they left marble, we may say that where they found a rude block they left a finished statue."

The Professor goes on to shew that Shakespeare when compared with Pope must be acknowledged to be less correct, though Pope may be represented in comparison with the great bard by one of Dr. Johnson's tropes which contrasts a genius " cutting a colossus from a rock with an artist carving heads on cherry stones." [2]

Virgil may be compared with Lucretius to shew on the one hand the smooth accurately carved statue, like the well-known portrait statues of Augustus, Tiberius, and Agrippina, and on the other a carelessness and want of

---

[1] He will tone down what is uneven, he will smooth rough places, yet he will take away all weakness, he will act like a player on the stage who is acting now a Satyr, now a rustic Cyclops.

[2] Conington's *Miscellaneous Writings*, vol. i. p. 4.

POETUS AND ARRIA.

technical skill such as we see in the early Greek statuary, the Hermes Criophorus at Wilton House, assigned to Calamis, or the Penelope in the Vatican, in which the hair of the one and the fingers of the other shew a disregard of nice technical skill, and which Cicero and Quintilian would probably have called hard and rigid.

Quis enim eorum, qui haec minora animadvertunt, non intelligit Canachi signa rigidiora esse, quam ut imitentur veritatem? Calamidis dura illa quidem, sed tamen molliora, quam Canachi.—Cic. *Brut.* xviii. 70.

Quint. *Inst. Or.* xii. 10. 7.—*Supra*, Essay i. 4.

An attempt of the poet may be traced throughout the lyrics of Horace to find a metre allowing variety of expression and melody combined with the strict observance of law which would be required by the Roman ear. But he found that the Latin language and the Roman legal prejudice could not be made to yield the necessary elasticity. He expresses his feeling on this point in the second ode of the fourth book, where he compares Pindar to a dashing sweeping torrent and himself to a careful bee working laboriously and neatly:

Monte decurrens velut amnis . . .
. . . . ruit profundo
Pindarus ore. . . .
Ego apis Matinae
More modoque

M

Grata carpentis thyma per laborem
Plurimum, circa nemus uvidique
Tiburis ripas, operosa parvus
Carmina fingo.[1]

And thus, while Horace could not find that free expression of thought or liberty of language would be acceptable to the Roman public, yet he knew that dexterity in handling a subject, and a refined mode of expression bound by strict law, were most popular. His work became what is sometimes called Dædalean, ingenious and correct, but not expressive of grander ideas than those of secular power and wealth. See Waldstein on *The Art of Phidias*, appendix iv., and throughout his essays, where he asserts that the highest part of the art of Phidias was not merely to make a neat fit, as we find stated by a learned Professor. See Mahaffy's *Rambles and Studies*, p. 90.

The catalogue of Greek forces enumerated in the second book of the *Iliad* when compared with that of the Italian troops in the seventh book of the *Æneid*, gives us some hints of the difference in taste between a Greek and a Roman poet. In Homer we find the Greek army repre-

---

[1] Pindar sweeps along like a torrent; I am like a bee laboriously threading the thyme blossoms, and stringing ingenious verses together in a toilsome manner.

sented as an organic body in groups, with the same lines separating all the different members. It is true that almost . every paragraph begins with the same words, proceeds with the same words, and ends with the same words :

οἱ δ' εἶχον . . . τῶν ἦρχε . . . τῷ δὲ ἕποντο.—*Il.* ii.

But here and there a striking point of the hero's history or of his country is mentioned, as in the cases of Philoctetes, and the central point of the poem, the wrath of Achilles and the wisdom of Ulysses, and the wealth and power of Agamemnon is mentioned. But in Virgil's descriptive catalogues there is no grouping or variety, the description rambles about, and if there be any feature pervading it, the mention of the names of leaders and their personal history is prominent rather than the places from which the men came or their numbers. When Hippolytus is mentioned the poet runs aside into a long legend which has no particular bearing on the Italian army.

The poetical finish of some of Virgil's touches, as in the similes where he compares the Sabine troops to the waves of the sea or the ears of a cornfield, is very fine, but both these and the comparison of the troop of Messapus to a flock of swans seem rather an embellishment than a striking illustration, and the whole catalogue in Virgil may be called

VENUS CAPITOLINA.

fine work, while Homer's catalogue is simple and powerful.   On the one side we have the powerful grandeur of the Parthenon sculpture, and on the other the confused battles of the triumphal arches and their ornamentation.

The tendency of the Roman mind towards exact technical description, without consideration of motives, can be traced again in Virgil's description of the games held by Æneas in memory of his father.   These are brought on the stage by the poet in the fifth book of the *Æneid*, and their characteristic features may be seen by a comparison with the games given by Achilles as described in the twenty-third book of the *Iliad*.   Virgil trusts more than Homer to a minute enumeration of the incidents by which each contest is attended, Homer states the reason for introducing them.   Homer's incidental events by which the encounters are affected have a simpler and less complicated aspect than those of Virgil.   Thus in the chariot race and in the ship race and in the boxing match the Roman applauds and gives most credit to brute strength.   Perhaps this is most remarkable in the boxing match, where the Herculean Entellus wins the fight from the more agile Dares.   Virgil exults in his power of painting the actual scene, Homer goes back to the occasion, and the motive idea.   The lines which give most prominence and

VENUS GENETRIX.

exaltation to Entellus describe his huge limbs, and the famous stroke of his fist.

> Et magnos membrorum artus, magna ossa lacertosque
> Exuit, atque ingens media consistit arena.—*Æn.* v. 422.
>
> Sternitur exanimisque tremens procumbit humi bos.—*Ib.* 481.

Dares is driven across the arena by his adversary's height and strength of arm.

> Praecipitemque Daren ardens agit aequore toto,
> Nunc dextra ingeminans ictus, nunc ille sinistra.
> *Æn.* v. 456

The merits of the description in Homer depend much more upon the straightforward simplicity of the way in which the match ends by one stroke which is not parried because the other combatant has not a quick eye :

> κόψε δὲ παπτήναντα παρήϊον· οὐδ' ἄρ' ἔτι δὴν
> ἑστήκειν.—*Il.* xxiii. 690.

This is followed by a striking simile comparing the fallen boxer to a fish thrown by the waves on the shore.

Another characteristic element of the descriptions of prize fights is that the supernatural element is brought in by Homer much more than by Virgil. Apollo and Athena both take part in the encounters, just as in the Greek sculptures and reliefs the gods interfere or help, while in the Roman reliefs, with few exceptions, human beings alone take part.

Turning from poetry to sculpture, we find that the kind of technical art which was naturally developed at Rome by the wealth and luxury of imperial society and by the national strictness was skill in the representation of mental feelings and desires by striking groups or forms in sculptures. The Greeks, of course, imitated the defects or the pains of the human body and their effects upon its form, for instance the famous statue of a lame man, probably Philoctetes,

Syracusis autem claudicantem cuius ulceris dolorem sentire etiam spectantes videntur.—Plin. *Nat. Hist.* xxxiv. 8, 19,

or the bust of Æsop, but they did not carry technical skill in this direction to the extent to which the Romans did in the busts of Seneca or the statues of Nero or of Commodus. Such representations would have been condemned by the best Greek taste as barbarous. We know from Lucian that the later Greek sculptors, Demetrios and others, did make exact likeness even of deformities their aim, and in this the Roman realistic sculptors followed them :

Σὺ δὲ εἴ τινα παρὰ τὸ ὕδωρ τὸ ἐπιρρέον εἶδες προγάστορα, φαλαντίαν, ἡμίγυμνον τὴν ἀναβολήν, ἠνεμωνέμον τοῦ πώγωνος τὰς τρίχας ἐνίας, ἐπίσημον τας φλέβας αὐτοανθρώπῳ ὅμοιον, ἐκεῖνον λέγω.—Lucian, *Philopseud.*, 18.

Skill in overcoming the difficulties presented by the material upon which the artist had to work must of course be mentioned here, as characteristic of the Augustan school of art.   Pliny in several passages appears to think that the chief reason for admiring a group is that it has been carved out of a single block of marble.   He says in speaking of a Laocoon, and of a work by Pasiletes representing a lioness teased by cupids, that the figures were cut from a single block,

omnes ex uno lapide.—Plin. xxxvi. 5, 4,

shewing that the technical skill of the sculptor was one of the principal objects of admiration to his eye.

Besides the general tone of literature in imperial times, there was a popular practice which tended strongly to encourage the development of the feelings rather than of the understanding: I mean the general custom of recitation. In order to avoid the tedious dulness of which the satirists complain, recourse was had naturally to exciting rather than argumentative or thoughtful treatment of any subject.[1]

---

[1]   For easier 'tis to learn and recollect
What moves derision than what claims respect.
                              Hor. *Ep.* ii. 1, 263.
But a man who is over nice is apt to destroy the very thing he aims at, especially when he is trying to recommend himself by metre and art, for people are more ready to like the fanciful and to remember it than what merits their approval and veneration.

The subject itself also suffered of course, and everything like political economy, natural science, statistics, or detail of facts was excluded. Yet the Romans liked statistical details as facts without exerting their minds to draw conclusions from them.

The endeavour made by Roman workers in metal to produce medallions of extraordinarily delicate work may be seen by reference to books in which Roman medallions are described. One class of medallions was that of ornaments formed for personal decoration, of which we have hundreds of different types. Some of these are distinguishable by having holes bored in them for suspension, or by other modes of fastening them to the dress of the wearer. Another class was intended to shew the great powers of the artificer who could attach together parts of one medal which were of different metals. Thus we find a circle of silver ornament surrounding a centre of bronze, or a golden edge surrounding a silver coin.[1]

Subjects taken from daily life were also of course, a part of what we may call technical art, which the luxury of the Romans developed in a greater degree than it had been practised by the Greeks. But still it would not be fair to the Greeks not to mention some works designed by them

---

[1] Froehner, pp. xii. xiv. xv.

APOLLO BENDING BOW.

which are known to us, such as the Astragalizontes of Polycleitus or the Spinario.

Fecit et quem canona artifices vocant, lineamenta artis ex eo petentes veluti a lege quadam, solusque hominum artem ipsam fecisse artis opere iudicatur ; fecit et destringentem se et nudum talo incessentem, duosque pueros item nudos talis ludentes, qui vocantur astragalizontes, et sunt in Titi imperatoris atrio.—Plin. xxxiv. 8, 19.

These may be taken as instances of the knowledge the Greeks had that such representations were admired, though the mind of the Greek not having been degraded by wealth, the admirers of these were few. The figures of boys, mentioned by Pliny, were probably useful supports or ornaments.

This is only a part of the large subject which may be called the individualism or love of personality which the Romans shewed in their works of art, and which led them to carry individual portraiture much further than the Greeks ever did in busts and statues. Many of these busts are exact likenesses of the original, and not ideal representations, as were those of Lysippus. This peculiarity of Roman sculpture has been made the subject of my first essay. See also above.

The influence of wealth upon Roman art as compared with Greek may also be noticed in other ways. For instance, many passages of the *Æneid* and *Iliad*, of which the following are very striking, may be observed.   Homer, in *Il.* ix. 213, gives a long description of the cooking of the heroes' meal, beginning with the killing of the animals, the lighting of the fire, and the spitting of the joints, while Virgil only applies, in *Æn.* v. 100, two or three lines to the cooking of the meal.   This indicates the desire of the poet not to shock his patrons' aristocratic notions of a meal by going too far into particulars.   Again, in the tenth book of the *Æneid*, Virgil has three lines describing the treasures offered to Æneas of works of silver and ingots of gold, while Homer, speaking of a similar offer, only enumerates bronze, gold, and wrought iron generally.   Seneca with Stoic cynicism criticises this Roman fault :

Quaerimus non quale sit quidque, sed quanti.—*Ep.* 115, 10 ;[1]

and says that the number of statues and their expense was valued more than their beauty or their historical interest.

It may be seen, by comparing some of the modern poets with the more early in English literature, how the imperial influence of England has affected them in the same way as it affected the Roman poets and sculptors.   Take the

---

[1] Cf. Sen. *Ep.* 41, 5.

following passage, describing the beauty of Iseult, from Mr. Swinburne's *Tristram and Iseult*, and see how he attempts to bring out all the smaller details in many features of the woman, while those quoted from Spenser, Milton, and Wordsworth are content with single remarks which tell more than a confused catalogue. In the same way Virgil and Statius can be found to differ, and Lessing, in the *Laocoon*, has quoted a striking instance from a later Greek poet named Manasses, who when compared with Homer exhibits an example of the two extremes, Homer having uttered nothing in description of Helen, though Manasses has lavished many lines upon her :

> The very veil of her bright flesh was made
> As of light woven and moonbeam-coloured shade
> More fine than moonbeams ; white her eyelids shone
> As snow sunstricken that endures the sun,
> And through their curled and coloured clouds of deep
> Luminous lashes, thick as dreams in sleep,
> Shone as the sea's depth swallowing up the sky's
> The springs of unimaginable eyes.
> As the wave's subtler emerald pierced through
> With th' utmost heaven's inextricable blue,
> And both are woven and molten in one sleight
> Of amorous colour and implicated light,
> Under the golden guard and gaze of noon,
> So glowed their aweless amorous plenilune,
> Azure and gold and ardent grey, made strange
> With fiery difference and deep interchange

VENUS ANADYOMENE.

> Inexplicable of glories multiform ;
> Now as the sullen sapphire swells toward storm
> Foamless, their bitter beauty grew acold,
> And now afire with ardour of fine gold.
>
> Swinburne's *Tristram and Iseult.*

Spenser says of Una:

> One day, nigh wearie of the yrkesome way,
> From her unhastie beast she did alight ;
> And on the grass her dainty limbs did lay
> In secrete shadow, far from all men's sight ;
> From her fayre head her fillet she undight
> And layd her stole aside : her angel's face,
> As the great eye of heaven, shyned bright
> And made a sunshine in the shady place ;
> Did never mortal eye behold such heavenly grace.

And again of Alma:

> For shee was faire, as faire mote ever bee,
> And in the flowre now of her freshest age ;
> Yet full of grace and goodly modestie
> That even heaven rejoiced her sweete face to see.
>
> *Faerie Queene*, book i. cant. iii. iv.

Milton, speaking of Adam and Eve, has the following short descriptions :

> His fair large front and eye sublime declared
> Absolute rule : and hyacinthine locks
> Round from his parted forehead manly hung
> Clustering, but not beneath his shoulders broad.

And of Eve:

> To whom thus Eve, with perfect beauty 'dorned.
> > *Paradise Lost,* book iv.

Wordsworth says of his wife:

> She was a phantom of delight
> When first she gleamed upon my sight ;
> A lovely apparition sent
> To be a moment's ornament ;
> Her eyes as stars of twilight fair ;
> Like twilight too her dusky hair ;
> But all things else about her drawn
> From Maytime and the cheerful dawn :
> A dancing shape, an image gay,
> To haunt, to startle, and waylay.

and after some more beautiful lines, he ends with

> A spirit, yet a woman too.

and

> And yet a spirit still, and bright
> With something of angelic light.
> > *Poems of the Imagination,* viii.

In a translation of Michel Angelo's sonnets, Wordsworth says :

> 'Tis sense, unbridled will, and not true love
> That kills the soul ; love betters what is best,
> Even here below, but more in heaven above.
> > *Miscellaneous Sonnets,* xxv.

N

In connection with the above biographical and personal characters of Roman portraiture in art, we may notice the human feeling which is expressed in Roman poetical scenes. Virgil has scenes of much pathetic interest. Thus the group of Mezentius wounded by the spear of Æneas but rescued by his son Lausus, who rushes in when Æneas is about to stab his father, and wards off the sword-thrust, thereby saving his father but losing his own life, rises to a grand height of pathos :—

> Iamque assurgentis dextra plagamque ferentis
> Aeneae subiit mucronem, ipsumque morando
> Sustinuit.   Socii magno clamore sequuntur,
> Dum genitor nati parma protectus abiret.
>
> *Æn.* x. 797.

Then after Æneas has killed Lausus, the picture of the wounded father Mezentius in desperate grief is touching :

> Nunc vivo, neque adhuc homines lucemque relinquo,
> Sed linquam.   Simul hoc dicens attollit in aegrum
> Se femur, et, quanquam vis alto volnere tardat
> Haud deiectus equum duci iubet.   Hoc decus illi,
> Hoc solamen erat, bellis hoc victor abibat
> Omnibus.   Alloquitur maerentem et talibus infit :
> Rhoebe, diu, res si qua diu mortalibus ulla est,
> Viximus.—*Æn.* x. 855.

We have attitudes of the body used to show feelings of the mind, just as we before had formations of the features.

The Roman love of realistic statement of facts as seen in external nature is shown by Lucretius in his description of the Athenian plague, in which he writes with painful accuracy of the symptoms, and the hideous and filthy aspect of the patient's body, the bloodshot eyes and ulcered throat, and fetid breath. Even the sad brow, maddened expression, compressed nostrils, and hollow temples are enumerated with Roman realism and disregard of the sickening picture thus brought into view. The poet's imitation of Thucydides is thus rendered almost disgusting, by the Roman tendency of his mind to insist upon actual life-like pictures. Here and there, however, we must confess that Lucretius gives exquisitely artistic scenes. Most statuesque descriptions in his poem are that of the enraptured gaze of Mars on the beauty of Venus,

> Pascit amore avidos, inhians in te, dea, visus.
> *De Rer. Nat.* i. 36,

and of the babe just born,

> Tum porro puer, ut saevis proiectus ab undis
> Navita, nudus humi iacet infans.
> *De Rer. Nat.* v. 222.

In the Capitol at Rome stood statues of all the seven kings, as we learn from Pliny, who in the same part of his *Natural History* gives some statements about the early history of portrait statues:

N 2

Togatae effigies antiquitus ita dicabantur.   Placuere et nudae tenentes hastam ab epheborum e gymnasiis exemplaribus, quas Achilleas vocant.   Graeca res nihil velare, at contra Romana ac militaris thoracas addere.   Caesar quidem dictator loricatam sibi dicari in foro suo passus est ; nam lupercorum habitu tam noviciae sunt, quam quae nuper prodiere paenulis indutae.   Mancinus eo habitu sibi statuit, quo deditus fuerat.—*Nat. Hist.* xxxiv. 5, 10.

Seneca claims the credit of having advanced this department of art as due to imperial Rome:

Multum egerunt, qui ante nos fuerunt, sed non peregerunt, suspiciendi tamen sunt et ritu deorum colendi.   Quidni ego magnorum virorum et imagines habeam incitamenta animi et natales celebrem ? Quidni ego illos semper honoris causa adpellem ?—*Ep.* 64, 9.

Silius Italicus gives a description of Scipio's features as expressive of the powers of the great hero,

Martia frons, facilesque comae, nec pone retroque
Caesaries brevior, flagrabant lumina miti
Adspectu, gratusque inerat visentibus horror.
Pun. viii. 559.

Plutarch also, as before remarked, in his biographical sketches of Pompey and Cicero, remarks upon their personal appearance as part of their character.   He says of Pompey that he had an imperial face like Alexander,[1] and of Cicero that he was lean and fleshless, ἰσχνὸς καὶ ἄσαρκος.

---

[1] Plut. *Pom.* ii.

Even Æneas is represented as pitying the rash courage of the youth, Lausus, and though he has killed him as an enemy yet he groans deeply,

> Ingemuit miserans graviter, dextramque tetendit,
> Et mentem patriae subiit pietatis imago.—*Æn.* x. 823.

The group of Dido and her sister at the end of the fourth book of the *Æneid* is not less pathetic :

> Sic fata gradus evaserat altos,
> Semianimemque sinu germanam amplexa fovebat
> Cum gemitu, atque atros siccabat veste cruores.
> Illa gravis oculos conata attollere, rursus
> Deficit ; infixum stridit sub pectore volnus.
> Ter sese attollens cubitoque adnixa levavit
> Ter revoluta toro est, oculisque errantibus alto
> Quaesivit caelo lucem, ingemuitque reperta.—*Æn.* iv. 685.

Dido's character and high spirit are painted by Virgil very powerfully. Her passionate despair and indignation is far above the wild impulse of most female characters represented in ancient poetry, as those of Medea or Phædra. Virgil has created a heroic figure in Dido, expressed in great measure by the movements and attitudes of her body, which in pathetic situation and action equals even the

Homeric and Attic heroines, Andromache, Penelope, or Cassandra.

In the writings of Lucilius we find an early stage of some of the Roman biographical tendencies which became afterwards much more prominent in Roman literature and art. In the first place he evidently lived and spoke about some of the great men of his day.   Horace describes his intimate friendship with Lælius and Scipio Africanus, and says that these two heroes used to play with him,

> Nugari cum illo et discincti ludere, donec
> Decoqueretur olus, soliti.—*Sat.* ii. 1, 73.

Scipio Africanus minor is distinguished by Lucilius with the epithet great (Lucil. xi. 10), and Lælius is called wise in the famous passage quoted by Cicero—

> O lapathe, ut iactare necesse est, cognitu' cui sis
> In quo Laeliu' clamores σοφός ille solebat
> Edere compellans gumias ex ordine nostros.
>
> *Fin.* II. 8, 24.

ESSAY V.

ROMANO-GREEK ARCHITECTURE.

In the Aventine hill, under the monastery of S. Saba, there is a vast subterranean quarry, from which carts may often be seen at the present day carrying blocks of a reddish-brown stone to the various quarters of Rome, wherever new buildings happen to be in the course of erection. The stone obtained from this quarry is the harder kind of tufa, of which a great part of the hills of Rome consist.[1] It naturally became the building stone used by the first founders of Rome, and is found in all the most ancient fragments of masonry which still remain. In many places, as on the cliffs of the Alban lake, and the sides of many of the hillocks in the Campagna, this stone may be seen presenting, when partially decayed, a very considerable likeness to a

---

[1] See *Rome and the Campagna*, R. Burn, 1871, chap. ii. p. 15.

wall of horizontal layers of stone. When quarried, it naturally breaks into rectangular blocks, and suggests of itself that mode of building which we find actually to exist in the earliest efforts of Roman builders.

The most interesting of such primæval relics is a fragment of wall which skirts the west end of the Palatine hill, and is assigned by M. Braun to the earliest enclosure of that hill, the so-called Roman Quadrata of Dionysius :[1]

μέγα δὲ τούτου τεκμήριον ὅτι τῆς τετραγώνου καλουμένης Ῥώμης ἦν ἐκεῖνος ἐτείχισεν, ἐκτός ἐστιν.—ii. 65.

The blocks in this wall are arranged in layers placed alternately parallel to and across the line of the wall (headers and stretchers), so as to bind the mass together firmly. No mortar is used, and the joints are fitted so accurately as to shew a more considerable knowledge of the art of masonry than we should expect at so early a period. It seems on this account questionable whether the usually received opinion as to the antiquity of this wall can be correct, and the fragments of the wall of Servius Tullius (B.C. 578—535) found on the sides of the Aventine and the Quirinal

---

[1] *Ann. dell' Inst.* 1852, p. 324; *Mon. dell' Inst.* vol. v. tav. 39, 50; *R. and C.* chap. iii. pp. 34, 41.

hills are perhaps more deserving of attention as undoubtedly ancient works.[1] In these fragments of the Servian wall the art of building appears in a more imperfect state than in that on the Palatine. The vertical joints are not so carefully arranged, and are often allowed to stand immediately one over the other, so as to impair the solidity of the masonry. The stones are placed close against the side of the hill, and in some places the lowest layers of them are imbedded in the natural rock.

The hills of Rome and of the Campagna being mostly low, and not offering in their natural state a sufficient defence, were frequently cased in this way with walls, which either abutted immediately upon the natural rock, as on the Quirinal, or were placed at a slight interval, which was filled up with rubble, as at Algidum near Præneste.[2] Other specimens of these rectangular horizontal tufa walls which belonged to cities destroyed during the Regal period, and therefore of indubitable antiquity, are to be seen in the neighbourhood of Rome. Such are the walls of Apiolæ destroyed by Tarquinius Priscus, situated on the right

---

[1] *R. and C.* chap. iv. pp. 44, 47, 50 ; *Ann. dell' Inst.* 1855, plates xxi.-xxv.   [2] Gell, *Top. Rom.* p. 42.

hand of the Via Appia at the tenth milestone from
Rome, and of Politorium, now La Giostra, near Castel
di Leva on the Via Ardeatina.[1]

> Bellum primum cum Latinis gessit et oppidum ibi Appiolas vi
> cepit. (Sc. Tarquinius).—Liv. i. 35.

In the walls of Tusculum and of Ardea, and many
other places in the Campagna, the same mode of
construction may be seen.[2]

As has been already mentioned, this style of building
is the natural product of the peculiar parallel cleavage
of the tufaceous rocks. Accordingly, wherever the
prevailing stone of the district is other than tufa, this
horizontal work is not found, and we see instead of it
in the more ancient walls the polygonal, or, as it was
called in Greece, the Cyclopean or Pelasgic style. It
has sometimes been assumed that polygonal structure
indicates a higher degree of antiquity than horizontal.
This, however, is not the case ; for the style of building
depends principally upon the nature of the material,
and some of the polygonal walls in Latium, as those
of the Temple of Fortune, built by Sulla at Præneste,

[1] Gell, pp. 87, 281 ; see *R. and C.* chap. xiv.
[2] *Ibid. Top. Rom.* pp. 432, 98.

belong to the time of the later Republic.[1] These later polygonal walls are easily distinguishable from the earlier by the greater accuracy of the joints, and the workmanlike style of the masonry. In the most ancient walls, as in some parts of those of Medullia, Alatrium, Artena Volscorum, and Signia, the joints are filled up with small stones, while in the later polygonal masonry the stones are closely fitted and selected with great care so as to present a flat surface.[2]

Of the most ancient kinds of gates, anterior to the discovery of the arch, no remains have been found at Rome ; but in the Campagna there are several curious and interesting varieties of ante-historic gateways. Sometimes, as at Olevano and Alatri, they are composed of a large horizontal slab placed upon two

---

[1] See note in Dennis, *Etruria*, vol. ii. p. 29. Dennis acknowledges the influence of local materials on the style of masonry, but does not think that it amounts to a constructive necessity. See a paper by Mr. Bunbury in the *Classical Museum*, vol. ii. p. 145.

[2] Gell, pp. 314, 111 ; *Monumenti dell' Inst.* 1829, plates i. ii. iii. ; Dodwell, *Pelasgic Remains*, p. 92. The walls of Tiryns are of this loose polygonal masonry. See Schliemann's *Ithaka und Troja*, p. 108. Leipzic, 1869. Dodwell, *Pelasgic Remains*, p. 124 ; Dionigi, *Viaggio in Lazio*. Fragments of this kind of work are to be seen in the Via di Casciano, and at the so-called villa of Cassius near Tivoli, and also at Arpino and Ferentino. See Nibby, *Analisi*, tom. i. 397, iii. 226.

vertical side posts ; sometimes these side supports are
slanted inwards, as in the gateway now to be seen
at Signia ;[1] and sometimes a kind of pointed arch is
formed by making each block of stone project a little
beyond the one upon which it rests, till the uppermost
stones meet. The most perfect specimen of this third
kind of gate is found at Arpino, and closely resembles
the well-known gate of Mycenæ. A single instance of
such a mode of construction is found at Rome in the
vault of the old well-house of the Capitol called the
Tullianum, the lower part consisting of overlapping
horizontal blocks which formerly met in a conical roof,
but are now truncated and capped with a mass of stones
cramped together with iron.[2] The Tullianum must
therefore be considered to be the earliest specimen of
building, other than simple wall constructions, now
extant in Rome, and probably anterior to the Cloaca
Maxima, in which we find the principle of the arch
already fully developed. If we may draw an inference
from the most ancient gateways of Etruria and the
rest of Latium,[3] the gates of Roma Quadrata on the

---

[1] See *Annali dell' Inst.* 1829, p. 78 ; *Monumenti dell' Inst.* tav. i. ii. iii.

[2] See *R. and C.* chap. vi. p. 81. There is a precisely similar well-
house at Burinna in Cos. See Reber, *Gesch. der Baukunst*, S. 222.

[3] As at Volaterræ, Fæsulæ, and Cora : Abeken, *Mittelitalien*, p. 159.

Palatine were not bare openings in the line of wall, but consisted of a square chamber with two doors, the one opening inwards and the other outwards. It seems probable that the Temple of Janus was a modification of such a gateway chamber; for as a part of the pomœrium these gateways would naturally be held sacred, and as the starting point of all expeditions beyond the city walls would be placed under the protection of Janus, the god who presided over the beginning of undertakings.[1] The inner door had the advantage of offering a second point of resistance to any besieging force which might have stormed the outer; and a further means of defence was usually provided for the gate by the construction of a projecting bastion on the right-hand side, from which the unshielded side of the attacking troops might be assailed with missiles. The gates of Norba and of Alba Fucensis shew defences of this nature.[2]

Of the general aspect of the city of Rome during the first years of its existence we can, of course, form only a conjectural notion. It probably consisted of an irregular collection of thatched cottages, similar to that

---

[1] See *R. and C.* chap. vi. p. 87.
[2] Abeken, *Mittelitalien*, p. 160; Vitruv. i. 5, 2.

shewn in later times as the Casa Romuli on the Palatine, among which were interspersed a few diminutive chapels, such as that of Jupiter Feretrius, which, even after its enlargement by Ancus, was not more than fifteen feet in length,[1]

ἔτι γὰρ αὐτοῦ σώζεται ἀρχαῖον ἴχνος ἐλάττονας ἢ πέντε ποδῶν καὶ δέκα τὰς μείζους πλευρὰς ἔχων.— Dionys. ii. 34.

Omnes ante me auctores secutus, A. Cornelium Cossum tribunum militum secunda spolia opima Jovis Feretrii templo intulisse exposui.—Liv. iv. 20.

Haec templi est origo, quod primum omnium Romae sacratum est.—Liv. i. 10 ;

the modest house of Numa, the curia of Hostilius, the so-called auguraculum, and the Temple of Jupiter Stator :[2]

> Quae nunc aere vides stipula tunc tecta videres
> Et paries lento vimine textus erat.
> Hic locus exiguus qui sustinet atria Vestae
> Tunc erat intonsi regia magna Numae.[3]—*Fast.* vi. 263.

Tufa walls with wooden supports were employed even in the more important buildings.

---

[1] *R. and C.* chap. viii. p. 192.   [2] *Ibid.* chap. viii. pp. 83, 103, 195.
[3] Where you now see roofs of metal you then might see thatch, and their walls were merely twisted osiers. This small spot which now has the halls of Vesta upon it, was then a great palace to bearded Numa.

We are assured, by the almost unanimous testimony of Roman historians, that the Tarquinii first introduced that great invention in building which the Roman engineers and architects carried, in later times, to the highest possible perfection, and which became the great glory of Roman masonry, the round arch.

Plebs traducebatur et ad alia opera, Cloacamque Maximam receptaculum omnium purgamentorum urbis sub terram agendam.—Liv. i. 56.

ἤρξατο δὲ καὶ τὰς ὑπονόμους ὀρύττειν τάφρους δι' ὧν ἐπὶ τὸν Τίβεριν ὀχεύεται πᾶν τὸ σύρρεον ἐκ τῶν στενώπων ὕδωρ, ἔργα θαυμαστὰ καὶ κρείττω λόγου κατασκευασάμενος.—Dion. iii. 67.

Praeterea cloacas mirabantur (senes Milonis aetate) opus omnium dictu maximum.[1]—Plin. N. H. xxxvi. § 24.

In Assyria and in Egypt the arch had long been used in subterranean buildings. The palaces at Nimrud contain several instances of arch structures, and round arches are used in the older Egyptian tombs.[2] But it is a strange fact in the history of architecture, that while we find the western branches of the great

---

[1] Everybody admires the sewers, which are a work greater than all the rest.

[2] Wilkinson, *Ancient Egyptians*, vol. iii. chap. 10, places the invention of the arch in Egypt 2020 B.C., and gives numerous instances of its very early use. See also Layard, *Nineveh and Babylon*, 1853, vol. i. p. 163; *Nineveh and its Remains*, vol. ii. p. 260.

Pelasgian family settled in Central Italy possessed of
a full knowledge of the principle of the arch, the eastern
or Hellenic branch appear to have been still ignorant of
it, or unwilling to employ it, during the period when

CLOACA MAXIMA.

their architecture was carried to the highest pitch of
perfection in other respects.

Whether the early inhabitants of Central Italy obtained
their knowledge of this most important principle in building by tradition from Eastern ancestors, or whether they

discovered it independently for themselves, cannot be determined. Greece, at all events, cannot claim the credit of having led the way to the frequent employment of the arch in building. In whatever way the principle was introduced into Italian architecture, it must have made great progress in early times ; and the fact that the tufa stone, commonly used for buildings not exposed to the outer air, could be so easily split or cut into suitable wedge-shaped masses, contributed not a little to the rapid development of this architectural contrivance. Another cause which has also been justly assigned for the great perfection to which the art of subterranean tunnelling and vaulting arrived in Etruria and at Rome in very early times, was the necessity for regulating the floods to which the valleys of the Arno and Tiber are peculiarly subject, and of draining the pestilential swamps or maremmas of the coasts of Latium and Tuscany. Works like the Cloaca Maxima and the great canal on the bank of the Marta, first described by Dennis, were indispensable as soon as it became desirable to occupy the lower grounds of these districts. Such considerations may diminish our surprise at finding so gigantic a work as the Cloaca undertaken at so early a period of the history of Rome ; [1] and we cannot

---

[1] See *R. and C.* chap. xii. pp. 280, 283.

but observe that the description given by Dennis of the canal at the mouth of the Marta seems to be a strong confirmation of the much-disputed authority of Livy and Dionysius, when they ascribe the construction of the Cloaca to the Etruscan Tarquinii. The very name Tarquinii belongs to the town at the mouth of the river Marta ; and not only is the canal arched over in the same style with enormous red tufa blocks, but the side of the river at its mouth is protected by an embankment, which seems the very counterpart of the " pulchrum litus " at the mouth of the Cloaca Maxima. The width of the Marta canal is not inferior to that of the Cloaca, the span of its arch being fourteen feet, while the stones employed are far larger.[1] But though in the time of the Tarquins the principle of the arch was so thoroughly understood, yet it was not very widely used at Rome till a much later time. The specus of the Aqua Appia (B.C. 312), lately discovered near the Porta Maggiore, is not arched over, but has a gable-shaped covering, formed by two flat stones inclined at an acute angle to each other. Nor is the mouth of the emissary at the Alban lake, which was built at the end of the Veientine War (B.C. 396), formed by an arch, but by a large horizontal block, which shews, by the slanting manner in which the

---

[1] Dennis, *Etruria*, vol. i. p. 393.

ends are cut, a rude application of the principle of the arch. These two instances prove clearly that even in subterranean works, where the arch was most useful and most easily constructed, it was not always employed in the period of the early Republic. Still less was the invention of the arch applied at this time to the construction of public buildings. The great public building of the later Regal period, the Temple of the Capitoline Jupiter, was built on the normal plan of Tuscan temples, with columns and horizontal architraves. Its appearance was flat and low,[2] the breadth being nearly equal to the length, the intervals between the columns very wide, the architrave of wooden beams, and the wooden gable-ends built with a low pitch.[3]

Of the so-called Tuscan style, as described by Vitruvius, we have no ancient specimens left.[4] It was, in fact, the Italian contemporary of the Greek Doric, and its peculiarities consisted rather in the proportion which the several parts of the building bore to each other, than in any constructive difference. The columns were nearly of the

---

[1] Hirt, *Gesch. der Baukunst*, ii. S. 108. [2] Virtruv. iii. 2.

[3] See *R. and C.* chap. viii. p. 189.

[4] Winckelmann, however (œuvres, tom. ii. p. 575), mentions a Tuscan column as existing at the emissary of the Fucine lake. He also cites an Etruscan vase figured in *Dempst. Etrur.* tom. i. tab. 7, which represents Etruscan columns.

same height in both the orders, but in the Tuscan they
rested upon a base which was generally omitted in Doric
architecture.   The shafts were coarsely and superficially
fluted, and the capital rather less ornamental in the Tuscan
than in the Doric order, having one annulet only instead of
three under the capital (see *R. and C.* Fig. 1 and Fig. 2).
One principal characteristic of the Tuscan style was the
position of the columns at wide intervals from each other
(aræostyle), an arrangement which was hardly possible,
unless wooden beams were employed for the architrave,
the difficulty of obtaining stones of the requisite length
being insurmountable.   We know from Vitruvius that the
Temple of Ceres, near the Circus, first built seventeen
years after the expulsion of the kings, was a Tuscan
temple, with wide intervals between the columns, and
three cellæ similar to the Capitoline Temple:[1]

In araeostylis autem. . . . . . Tuscanico more, uti est ad Circum
Maximum Cereris et Herculis Pompeiani, item Capitolii.[2]—iii. 5.

[1] *R. and C.* chap. xii. p. 292.   The Temple of Juno at Elis had
originally wooden columns and architrave, and resembled the Tuscan
temples : ἐν δὲ τῷ ὀπισθοδήμῳ δρυὸς ὁ ἕτερος τῶν κιόνων ἐστί.—Paus. v. 16.
Hirt, *Gesch.* vol. iii. S. 5.

[2] In the temples where the columns are wide apart, after the Tuscan
fashion, as we find it in the temple of Ceres and Hercules, near the
Circus Maximus.

and it is just possible that the columns in the walls of
S. Maria in Cosmedin, which are placed at unusual distances from each other, may have belonged to the Imperial
restoration of this temple in the old fashion. Other
characteristics of the Tuscan style were the wooden architraves, and the rough projecting ends of the cross beams,
which corresponded to the Doric triglyphs. The ornaments
of the pediment and gable were adapted to this rude
structure. They usually consisted of pottery roughly gilt
or painted.

Propter quae Numa rex septimum conlegium figulorum instituit.[1]—
Plin. *N. H.* xxxv. § 46.

The old Tuscan style must not be considered as the
peculiar production of the district between the Tiber and
the Arno. It was in reality descended from the same root
as the Greek Doric, and stood in the same relation to that
style as the Italian section of the Pelasgic stock to the
Hellenic section. But after the year B.C. 496, fourteen
years after the expulsion of the kings, a more direct
influence began to be exerted on Roman art by the Greeks

---

[1] For this, the encouragement of pottery ware, the king, Numa,
created a seventh guild, that of potters.

of Lower Italy and Sicily.[1]   Pliny, speaking of the decorations of the Temple of Ceres above mentioned, quotes Varro as his authority for stating that " before the time when that temple was built all the temples in Rome were wholly Tuscan."

Ante hanc aedem Tuscanica omnia in aedibus fuisse auctor et Varro.   (Cereris aedem).—Plin. *N. H.* xxxv. § 45.

Quam (Cereris aedem) A Postumius dictator voverat.

Tac. *Ann.* ii. 49.

The older Doric architecture, so characteristic of the Greek temples of Lower Italy and Sicily, as at Pæstum,

---

[1] " Il y a un style romain, mais on ne peut pas dire qu'il a existé un art romain.   Quand ils ont eu une architecture à eux, les Romains n'en ont point créé les éléments qu'ils empruntaient à l'architecture grecque, ils les ont seulement modifiés, altérés trop souvent, combinés quelques fois d'une manière nouvelle pour satisfaire des besoins qui leur étaient propres.   Ils n'ont créé que deux genres d'architecture : l'amphithéâtre, qui suppose les gladiateurs, et l'arc de triomphe, qui suppose le triomphe.   Or, le triomphe, comme le gladiateur, est exclusivement romain.   Mais ils ont imprimé aux divers genres de monuments adoptées par eux le caractère de leur génie et le sceau de leur grandeur."—Ampère, *Histoire Romaine à Rome,* vol. iv. p. 9.

The above passage fairly expresses the amount of merit due to the Romans as architects.   It should not, however, be forgotten that they were the first nation who employed the arch, both simple and vaulted, extensively in building, and thereby opened an entirely new field of architecture.   Their mistake was that they clung so long to the Greek style of decoration, which after the development of the arch had lost its original constructive meaning.

Syracuse, Agrigentum, and Selinus,[1] was not, however, introduced in a pure form into Rome, but modified by an admixture of the already prevalent Tuscan. The so-called Temple of Hercules at Cora, which, though

TEMPLE AT GIRGENTI.

built in later times, was probably a restoration of a very early temple, is a good specimen of the mixed style which thus arose. It has the Tuscan wide intervals between its columns, and the simple Tuscan capitals and bases,

---

[1] See Wilkins's *Syracuse, Girgenti, and Pæstum.*

combined with the Doric triglyphs and mutules. The metopes are left plain, and the cornice has lost its characteristic eavelike slope.[1]

In the columns of this Tusco-Doric style, as may be seen in the Doric columns and capitals of the Theatre of Marcellus and of the Coliseum, the Attic base, consisting of a plinth, lower torus, scotia, and upper torus, was usually employed ; the shaft was much more slender than in the Grecian Doric, and was only partially fluted, if at all, and a cima recta was substituted for the echinus of the capital. The position of the triglyphs and the proportions of the cornice were also considerably changed (see *R. and C.* Figs. 2 and 3), and the whole effect is less massive and bold than that of the Tuscan temples.[2]

The increasing influence of Doric forms of architecture also altered the ground-plan of the Roman temples considerably. The old square Etruscan temple, in which the

---

[1] Nibby, *Viaggio*, vol. ii. p. 208. This temple was carefully copied by Raphael when he was entrusted by Leo the Tenth with the strange design of the entire restoration of Rome on the ancient plan. See Fea on Winckelmann, tom. ii. p. 582, note, and ii. part. 2, p. 238. Winckelmann assigns the present temple at Cora to the time of Tiberius.

[2] Of the three Doric temples at Pæstum the large hypæthral temple is the oldest. " It has low columns with a great diminution of the shaft, bold projecting capitals, a massive entablature, and triglyphs placed in the angles of the zophorus."—Wilkins's *Pæstum*, p. 59.

width was nearly as great as the length, gave way to the more oblong form of the Greek temple, in which the length was nearly double of the breadth. It was necessary, if the wooden architraves were to be replaced by stone, that the intervals between the columns of the front should be diminished. But though the proportion of the sides was thus changed, the ancient Tuscan arrangement of the interior remained as before. Even down to the time of the Empire many of the Roman temples were still divided in the Tuscan fashion into two principal parts; the open portico in front, with the single, or double, or triple cella behind it. In the Roman Forum there were several temples exhibiting this arrangement, to which the name of prostylos was given by Vitruvius. The three ruins which now occupy so prominent a position at the northern end of the Forum, the Temples of Saturn, of Concord, and of Vespasian, were all of this kind. The Temple of Concord is especially remarkable for the union of a broad Tuscan cella with a narrow Greek portico;[1] and the Tuscan double-chambered plan may be also observed in the Temples of Jupiter and Juno, in the Porticus Octaviæ, as given in the Capitoline plan of Rome.[2] The Roman prostylos is in fact, as Professor Reber well remarks,

---

[1] See *R. and C.* chap. vi. p. 91.   [2] *Ibid.* chap. xiii. p. 307.

nothing else than a compromise between the old Tuscan temple and the newer Greek models.[1]

In the restorations of older temples by Augustus, the old square shape of the ground-plan was frequently retained on account of the difficulty of removing surrounding buildings ; and even where, as in the Temple of Venus and Rome, designed by Hadrian, the Greek peripteral temple was reproduced, the influence of old traditional forms may be traced in the breadth of the cella in proportion to its length, and in its conventional division into two instead of three compartments.[2]

An alteration peculiarly Roman was also made in the cella of the Greek temple. The Roman eye was offended by the naked walls of the Greek cella, and, with that want of perception of the true principles of art which marked the Roman architects, they proceeded to clothe them with pilasters and other decorations, which were totally without meaning in relation to the structure. Thus was formed the pseudo-peripteral temple, a weak imitation of the Greek peripteral (see Fig. 4).

The round form of temple was more affected by the Romans than by the Greeks, who used a circular shape only in their smaller monumental works, as in the choragic

---

[1] Reber, *Gesch. der Baukunst*, p. 400.

[2] See *R. and C.* chap. viii. p. 170.

monument of Lysicrates and the Temple of the Winds at
Athens. The difficulty of finding a suitable roof, the
necessarily contracted space of the cella, and the inartistic
curve of the architrave, probably deterred the Greek architects from employing this form of building. The well-
known round temple in the Forum Boarium at Rome,
usually called the Temple of Vesta, and the somewhat
similar temple of Tivoli, are the most familiar specimens
of Roman work. It has not been ascertained in what
manner the roof of these temples was constructed ;
whether, as in the monument of Lysicrates, it was a tent-
like conical roof, or a dome, and whether it rested on the
cella walls or on the architrave of the circular colonnade.
The domed roof of the Pantheon cannot be admitted as
decisive of this question, because it is nearly certain that
the Pantheon was originally intended to be a part of
Agrippa's baths, and was only by an afterthought converted
into a temple, and provided with the incongruous Corinthian
portico which forms its entrance.[1] The difficulty of the
roof was avoided in cases where, as in the octagonal portico
of the Church of S. Cosma e Damiano, formerly the Temple
of the Penates, a colonnade was dispensed with.[2]

The Ionic order became known and employed by the

---

[1] See *R. and C.* chap. xiii. p. 330. [2] *Ibid.* chap. viii. p. 163.

Romans early in the third century B.C. We find a strange mixture of the Ionic volute and dentil with the Doric triglyph and gutta in the tomb of Scipio Barbatus, now preserved in the Vatican Museum. This is the first monument upon which the Ionic volute appears at Rome, and it shows at how early a period the Romans had begun a practice, which was afterwards carried by them to such excess—the use of Greek architectural forms merely for decorative purposes, without structural meaning. A hundred years after the death of Scipio Barbatus, when the Macedonian wars of the second century B.C. had familiarised the Romans with Greek art, the Ionic order became well known in Rome, and the Ionic capital and column were used in many temples where the old Tuscan ground-plan was still retained. The Temples of Fortuna Virilis[1] and of Saturn,[2] and the exterior decorations of the Coliseum, illustrate the Roman treatment of the Ionic capital. In the first of these buildings we have a small pseudo-peripteral temple with Ionic half-columns, the shafts of which are cut in tufa and the capitals in travertine. As, however, travertine is too rough a material for the finer mouldings of the Ionic capital, recourse has been had to stucco to complete the decorative work. Marble was

---

[1] See *R. and C.* chap. xii. p. 289.   [2] *Ibid.* chap. vi. p. 93.

TEMPLE OF SATURN.

probably still a rare luxury when this temple was built, and therefore the architect had some excuse for this inartistic device.

The other peculiarity which we observe here is in the volutes of the corner capitals, which are turned outwards. It was the weak point of the Ionic order that the corner capitals could not be made to correspond with both the front and side capitals without this change.[1] The Greeks had already in most of their Ionic peripteral temples endeavoured to remedy this defect by making the corner volute project in the line of the diagonal instead of the line of the side of the building. This device is imitated in the Temple of Fortuna Virilis, and carried still further in the Temple of Saturn, where the volutes of all the capitals are placed diagonally instead of laterally (see *R. and C.* Figs. 5 and 6). The Ionic capital was deprived by this modification of its beautiful simplicity, and the peculiarity of its volutes was destroyed ; but on the other hand—what was of great use where poverty to imagine and incapacity

---

[1] Interesting specimens of the capitals and columns of Roman temples are now to be seen in some of the older churches and basilicas of Rome. The basilica of S. Lorenzo fuori le Mura is full of Ionic capitals of great variety and beauty. There are seven Ionic capitals and four Corinthian in the Church of S. Maria in Trastevere. Others may be seen in the Churches of S. Maria in Cosmedin, S. Stefano Rotondo, and S. Maria in Ara Cæli.

to adapt prevailed among architects, as at Rome—a model
form was gained applicable to any situation, and presenting
the same appearance on all sides. To the practical and
utilitarian Roman such considerations seem to have out-
weighed any regard for the principle, to which the Greeks
always adhered, of preserving in all cases the structural
meaning of their forms. In the work of Vitruvius, the
court architect of Augustus, this desire to reduce every
detail of architecture to fixed rules, in order to supply the
want of originality in design and taste in proportion,
appears on every page. But even Vitruvius protests
against the unmeaning employment of the Greek
decorative forms :

In Graecis operibus nemo sub mutilo denticulos constituit, non
enim possunt subtus cantherios asseres esse . . . . ea probaverunt
antiqui quorum explicationes in disputationibus rationem possunt
habere veritatis.[1]—iv. 2.

The Romans, however, not only thus disfigured the
Ionic capital of the Greeks, but failed in another point
essential to architectural excellence, in the conscientious
execution of details. The second range of capitals in the
Coliseum exemplifies this neglect very clearly. The

---

[1] In works done according to Greek fashion, no one ever places the
toothed mouldings above the brackets, for the ends of the supporting
rafters cannot be above the ornamental mouldings.

spirals of the volutes are there extremely shallow, the
curls are not completed, and the enrichment of the ovolo
is omitted.[1] In the Theatre of Marcellus this deterioration
of artistic feeling is not yet exhibited, and the Ionic
order there appears in its original Greek simplicity and
beauty.

With the introduction of marble as a building material[2]
came the general use of the Corinthian order in most
Roman temples of considerable size.   In Greece the
Corinthian capital was treated with great freedom and
variety, and its details not very strictly defined, nor was
it attempted on a large scale except under Roman
influences.[3]   In Rome itself the typical Corinthian
form became more fixed, in consequence of the above-
mentioned anxiety of the Roman artists to work by

---

[1] "Il faut savoir que les parties de cet édifice [the Coliseum] ne
sont pas trop exactement exécutées et que les moulures changent de
hauteur d'une place à l'autre."—Desgodetz, p. 110. A similar neglect
of the details of the capitals may be seen in the Corinthian and
composite orders of the grand Amphitheatre of El-Djemm (Thysdrus)
in Tunis. See *Ann. e Monum. dell' Inst.* 1852, p. 146.

[2] Probably about the time of Metellus Macedonicus, B.C. 143.

Hic idem (Metellus Macedonicus) primus omnium Romae aedem
ex marmore in iis ipsis monumentis molitus.—Vell. Peterc. i. 11, 5.

[3] The only extant Greek Corinthian building is the choragic
monument of Lysicrates at Athens.

pattern and rule in everything; and it soon outstripped the Doric and Ionic on account of its more general applicability and its alluring richness of ornamental detail. It is supposed that the first introduction of

CAPITALS OF COLUMNS.

this order into Rome was brought about by the barbarian act of Sulla, in transporting the columns of the Temple of Zeus at Athens to adorn his restoration of the Capitoline Temple of Jupiter.

P

Curam [of building up the Capitoline temple] victor Sulla suscepit, neque tamen dedicavit ; hoc solum felicitati ejus negatum.—Tac. *Hist.* iii. 72.

Of the remaining specimens of this order in Rome the portico of the Pantheon is probably the oldest. In that building the capitals appear somewhat shorter and broader than in the later examples in the porticoes of the temples of Castor (see *R. and C.* Fig. 7) and Vespasian in the Forum, and in the peristyle of Nerva's Forum.[1] Like the Ionic order, the Corinthian also suffered miserably at Rome, in some cases from the want of conscientious execution of its details. This is particularly remarkable in the foliations of the capitals of the Coliseum, in which the edges of the leaves are left smooth and plain, and the grooves and curves are made blunt and shallow.

The above-mentioned buildings contain the best-proportioned specimens of the Corinthian order. While the capital remains nearly the same in all the Roman examples, with the exception of a few trifling differences in the indentation of the leaves and the small central volutes, the base and cornice are varied in several instances ; the Attic base being introduced in the Temple of Antoninus and Faustina and in the Thermæ of Diocletian, and the cornice being without dentils in the former building,

---

[1] See *R. and C.* pp. 101, 136.

and in the Portico of Octavia.[1] Another remarkable modification of this order at Rome is to be seen in the ruins of the Forum of Nerva and in the Arch of Constantine. The columns are there placed in front instead of under the entablature, and connected with it by projections of ornamental work similar to the entablature.[2] More important variations from the normal structure are to be seen in the little temple at Tivoli, called the Temple of the Sibyl, marking a transit from the pure Corinthian to the composite order. The capitals in this building have their angular volutes so much enlarged that they might be easily mistaken for those of the composite order, and the second ring of acanthus leaves is diminished and almost hidden beneath the first; but the Corinthian character is preserved by the presence of the smaller central volutes. The leaves are remarkable for the very peculiar thistle-like mode in which their curves and indentations are cut, and the lotus flower over the centre is of a much larger size than in the ordinary Corinthian capital. The date of this

---

[1] See *R. and C.* pp. 113, 309.

[2] The temples of Baalbec, probably built by Hadrian, and those of Palmyra by Aurelian, are the most colossal ruins of the Roman Corinthian order. See Wood's *Baalbec and Palmyra:* London, 1753. The Church of S. Paolo at Naples, formerly the Temple of Castor, shows the projections in the entablature which occur in the Forum of Nerva. See *R. and C.* p. 136.

temple is uncertain. Nibby refers it to the period of Roman architecture between Sulla and Augustus, before the Greek rules of proportion were so completely recognised as at a later time.[1]

The composite capital, for it can hardly be called an order, as there is nothing in the entablature or the base to distinguish it from the Corinthian, was formed probably under the patronage of the first Emperors. The earliest instance we have of it now extant in Rome is in the Arch of Titus (see *R. and C.* Fig. 8) ; and there are only three other ruins where it is found. These are the Arch of Septimius Severus, the Arch of the Goldsmiths, and the Baths of Diocletian, where it is mixed up with Corinthian capitals. The peculiar combination of which it consists, the superposition of the Ionic volutes upon two rings of Corinthian acanthus leaves, is not generally considered a very happy artistic design. Hope says of it that "instead of being a new creation of genius it gave evidence of poverty to invent and ignorance to combine ;" and Fergusson is hardly less complimentary to the Roman architects.[2]

But though we must deny to this Roman adaptation of

---

[1] Nibby, *Viaggio*, vol. i. p. 159. See *R. and C.* chap. xiv. p. 397.

[2] Hope, *Essays on Architecture*, vol. i. p. 68 ; Fergusson, *Principles of Art*, p. 482.

Greek forms the credit of originality, or even of symmetry of design, yet its rich appearance was peculiarly suited to the lavish ornamentation with which the Roman emperors delighted to trick out their palaces and halls, and it well represents to us the character of the Roman Imperial architecture, with its indiscriminate combination of mouldings and profusion of gaudy detail.

We can trace the beginning of this faulty juxtaposition of incompatible forms even in the age of the revival of Greek architecture under Augustus and the earlier emperors, when, as we learn from Vitruvius, the strictest regard was in general paid to the Greek rules of proportion. Vitruvius himself complains of the Romans for not observing the golden principle of Greek architecture, that each exterior ornament must express some real part of the building :

Ita quod non potest in veritate fieri, id non putaverunt in imaginibus factum posse certam rationem habere.[1]—iv. 2.

Capitolii fastigium illud et ceterarum aedium non venustas sed necessitas ipsa fabricata est.—Cic. *De Or.* iii. 46.

And we find his strictures exemplified in several of the remaining temples in the Roman Forum. In the entablature of the temples of Castor, of Concord (a fragment

---

[1] And thus we see that the old architects thought that what could not really be so placed, ought not in mere imitations to be so placed.

of which may be seen in the corridor of the tabularium), and of Vespasian, belonging respectively to the reigns of Augustus, Tiberius, and Titus, and in the Thermæ of Diocletian (S. Maria degli Angeli), the mistake is committed of introducing into the cornice various ornaments which originally represented the same part of the wooden roof, and ought not therefore to be combined in the same building. It will be observed also that in the cornices of the temples of Vespasian and of Castor some of the ornamental work loses its significance by the incongruous mixture of designs.[1] Between the leaves of the so-called Ionic egg-moulding we have the original sprays or stalks of the leaves changed into meaningless arrow-heads. The curve of the upper moulding of the cornice, and other parts of the upper cornice, are overladen with rich foliated work, which, however elegant in itself, is quite misplaced in such a position.

This tendency to incongruous ornamentation shows itself also in the variety displayed in the fluted shafts of the Imperial times. Some of these have a beading inserted between the flutings, while others have half their length only fluted, or the upper half fluted in a different style from the lower. Spiral and even horizontal fluting

---

[1] See *R. and C.* chap. vi. pp. 101, 118.

was sometimes introduced, and occasionally a combination of the two. Connected with these strange displays of the Roman want of æsthetic perception of the beautiful in art was the effect necessarily produced by the use of foreign stone brought from all parts of the world. Huge granite columns from Egypt and ponderous blocks of African marble were constantly on their way up the Tiber to the Roman quays, where we still find them lying in profusion, as if too common to be worth removal into the great city, glutted as she then was with the spoils of half the world.[1]

> Aemulus illic
> Mons Libys Iliacusque nitent et multa Syene
> Et Chios et glauca certantia Doride saxa,
> Lunaque portandis tantum suffecta columnis.
>
> Statius, *Silv.* iv. 2, 26.[2]

These stones were often too hard to be cut into the requisite shapes, as in the case of granite or porphyry, or too richly veined and tinted to need other embellishment than their own bright hues and lovely shades of colour.

---

[1] On the different shapes—good, bad, and indifferent—introduced by way of variety into Roman architecture in Imperial times, see Winckelmann, *Essai sur l'Arch.* œuvres, tom. ii. p. 630.

[2] Here we have in rivalry the Libyan mountain and that of Ilium, and quantities of stones from Syene and Chios vying with the azure Dorian, and Luna, only just sufficient to supply the columns which are brought. (*R. and C.* p. 208.)

They were therefore cut in any way which was calculated
to show off their gorgeous brilliancy, without regard to the
rules of symmetry of proportion or beauty of form. Pliny
records a remark of Cicero when his attention was drawn
to a wall built of exquisitely variegated Chian marble as a
great work of art: " I should have thought much more of
it in that respect," said he, " if you had made stone from
Tibur (travertine) look as well as this does " :

Multo, inquit, ostenderunt cum lapicidinae Chiorum versicolores
istas maculas, M. Cicero, magis mirarer, si Tiburtino lapide
fecissetis.—*N. H.* xxxvi. § 46.

Not only innumerable marbles, but a great variety of
other stones enumerated by Pliny were used in the decoration of the Roman Imperial buildings. The French
excavations on the Palatine hill have lately discovered to
us the richness of design displayed in ornamenting the
palace of the Flavian emperors. At least a hundred
specimens of polished marble may be seen in the museum
there, of the most varied and beautiful colours, all of which
were collected in the ruins.[1]

Eo deliciarum venimus ut nisi gemmas calcare nolimus.—Seneca,
Ep. lxxxvi. 7.

Pavimenta ipsa lapide pretioso caesim diminuto varia picturae
genera discriminantur.—Apul. *Met.* v. 1.

---

[1] See *Cambridge Journal of Philology*, vol. ii. p. 88.

Thus, from the lack of purity of taste and a want of adherence to the natural and simple rules of art, the Roman buildings, clothed in their Greek dresses, too often show like the jackdaw in the fable tricked out with the peacock's feathers. The sneers of the great architect Apollodorus at the incongruity of the internal arrangement of Hadrian's masterpiece, the Temple of Venus and Rome, with its exterior pretensions, cost him his life ; but they were doubtless well deserved.[1]

Ἂν γὰρ αἱ θεαὶ, ἔφη, ἐξαναστήσεσθαι τε καὶ ἐξελθεῖν ἐθελήσωσιν οὐ δυνηθήσονται.—Dion. Cass. lx. 4.

The core of that temple was essentially Roman, consisting of huge vaulted roofs and hemispherical apses of brick, around which the Greek columnar structure was wrapped, as if to cover its nakedness. The Greek clothing of the interior of the Pantheon is another notable instance of such a hybrid composition. In all this the great deficiency of the Roman architects was, that they seemed blind to the majestic capacity for beauty of that great invention, the arch, which they themselves, from their peculiar circumstances, carried to such perfection, and applied to such a variety of

---

[1] See *R. and C.* chap. viii. p. 170.

practical objects. Their greatest buildings, such as the Coliseum, would have been much more dignified and noble had their designers omitted the unmeaning half-columns and capitals which are stuck on their sides, and left the noble rows of arches in their unadorned grandeur to tell their own tale.[1] No small part of the majesty of the Coliseum, as a ruin, is due to the fact that the bare arches of the interior are now, by the destruction of so large a portion of the exterior shell, exposed in their natural strength and simplicity. The Romans never seem to have taken that step in advance, afterwards made by the inventors of Gothic architecture, the development of the *decorative* capabilities of the arch.

Accordingly, in the decorative parts of their porticoes, palaces, and patrician residences, the Greek colonnade and horizontal entablature were chiefly used, and no skilful union of the useful with the ornamental was found. The great porticoes of the Campus Martius probably had flat entablatures and roofs, and were entirely Hellenic; so also were the exteriors of the

---

[1] The Septizonium was perhaps the worst instance of this kind of meaningless decoration. The Amphitheatre of Verona, on the contrary, has no columns, and shows a more simple taste.

palaces and houses on the Palatine and Esquiline.[1] That the Golden House of Nero was chiefly in the Greek style may be inferred from the enormous space it occupied. Hellenic architecture had no upper floors or stories, and therefore necessarily occupied a large area. This was natural in the Greek cities, where the population was not crowded, and space was easily obtained for extensions on the ground-floor. But if the requirements of an extragavant despot like Nero were to be satisfied after Greek models, and he was, according to his own fancy, to "be lodged as a man should be"—

Quasi hominem tandem habitare coepisse.—Suet. *Nero*, 31.

Reddita Roma sibi est, et sunt te praeside Caesar
Deliciae populi quae fuerant domini.—Mart. *Spec.* ii.

—an enormous area was necessary to provide for him. The descriptions we have of the Golden House show how this was carried out. Three colonnades of a mile in length formed the limits of the great Imperial folly;

---

[1] See *R. and C.* chaps. viii. and xiii. for illustrations. On the Campus were the Porticus Polæ, Porticus Europæ, Porticus Vipsania, Porticus Neptuni, Porticus ·Meleagri, Porticus Flaminia, &c., &c. Arches supported on columns were not commonly used till the time of Diocletian.

and it covered a great part of the Esquiline, the northern slope of the Cælian, the whole of the Coliseum valley, and the Velia as far as the Arch of Titus. Many parts of Hadrian's great villa near Tibur were not only built, but named after specific Greek buildings. He had a Poecile there, a Palæstra, a Lyceum, and a Prytaneum.[1]

At a much later date the vast palace of Diocletian at Spalatro exhibits still the same reluctance to resign the Greek decorative features, although their structural meaning is lost. The same ornamental network of columns and half-columns and pilasters is spread over the walls here, as in the older palaces of Rome.[2] Rows of triangular pediments, sometimes truncated, sometimes rounded, with other scattered and mangled limbs of the Greek façade, are here to be seen planted without meaning against the interior walls to break their extended flat surfaces. One great step, however, towards the artistic union of the column and arch, which the

---

[1] See Ligorio's description, Rome, 1751.

[2] The Thermæ of Diocletian at Rome (S. Maria degli Angeli) were the great repertorium whence the architects of the Renaissance borrowed the patterns for their niches with columns on each side, their broken cornices and pediments, and their rows of columns without entablatures.—Winckelmann, *Essai sur l'Arch.* tom. ii. p. 633.

want of genius for combination long prevented the Romans from making, is found in the palace of Diocletian. The spaces between the columns are bridged over by means of arches instead of flat entablatures; and thus colonnades are changed into arcades, and a union effected afterwards prolific of beautiful forms in modern architecture.

A step towards this had already been taken in the triumphal arches of the Romans; and yet their servile adherence to Greek forms of decoration, and the poverty of their invention, were not less glaringly displayed in that class of buildings. The triumphal arch could be claimed as a creation of the national warlike character:

Columnarum ratio erat attolli super ceteros mortales quod et arcus significant novicio invento.—Plin. *N. H.* xxxiv. § 27.

It was intended primarily to perpetuate the fame of a victorious general, to picture his exploits, and to raise his effigy above the rest of mankind. But though these arches are upon the whole some of the most successful efforts of purely Roman architecture, because the real and solid constructive parts occupy the most prominent place, yet Greek decorations are dragged in even here. The Romans placed an unmeaning front of pedestal, column, and capital, with abacus, frieze, and entablature, upon the surface of their massive piers of masonry, "thus tying, as the tyrant Mezentius did, the dead to the living."[1]

Mortua quin etiam jungebat corpora vivis
Componens manibusque manus atque oribus ora.

Virg. *Æn.* viii. 485.

The three great triumphal archways of Titus, Septimius Severus, and Constantine at Rome, and also the Arch of Drusus, are decorated with this foreign dress. In the Arch of Constantine alone the columns which stand in front are, in some measure, justified by the statues they support. Of the minor archways at Rome, that of Gallienus has Corinthian pilasters in the roughest style of art; the Janus Quadrifrons, in the Forum Boarium, probably once had rows of Corinthian columns between its niches, and the small gateway near it has decorative pilasters with composite capitals. On the other hand, the Arch of Dolabella, on the Cælian, which has a single line as cornice, and the Porta S. Lorenzo are examples of the impressive effect of a plain arch without Greek ornament. The Porta Maggiore

---

[1] Hope, *Essays on Architecture*, vol. i. p. 67. The first triumphal arch recorded is that of Stertinius, B.C. 196. Scipio Africanus and Fabius Maximus afterwards erected arches: see *R. and C.* chap. vi. p. 104. The whole number of ornamental arches at Rome was thirty-six: Preller, *Reg.* p. 234. Reber, *Gesch. der Bauk.* S. 424, gives a list of seventeen extant arches in Italy, France, Spain, and Africa.

may, perhaps, be classed with these ; but though it exhibits the sterling merits of Roman architecture in its massive rustic arches of travertine, it also shows the defects not less plainly. The unmeaning pediments and tasteless columns, with which the exterior is adorned, remind us of Pope's receipt for the front of a villa : " Clap four slices of pilaster on't ; that laid with bits of rustic makes a front."

The high stylobate or pedestal, placed under a column, first makes its appearance in the gateways and triumphal arches of the Imperial age. The Porta Maggiore and the Arch of Constantine afford specimens of columns so mounted, as it were, on stilts. The Temple at Assisi, and two Roman buildings at Palmyra, are cited by Winckelmann as the only cases in which separate stylobates are found in larger edifices.[1] These columns on pedestals were frequently imitated in the Renaissance period.

The idea of placing a statue upon the top of a column was, apparently, unknown to the Greeks ; or, at least, was never carried out by them on the immense scale of the two great Roman columns of Trajan and Marcus Aurelius. Such a mode of employing the column would have seemed strange to ancient Greek architectural ideas, in which a column was always used for the purpose of supporting a flat entablature. The column thus employed is, in fact,

---

[1] See Piranesi, *Magn. de Rom.* tab. 38, Fig. 1.

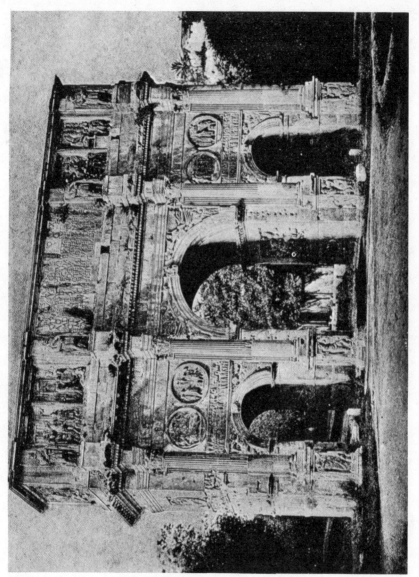

ARCH OF CONSTANTINE.

nothing more than a huge pedestal, which must necessarily be out of all proportion to the statue it carries on its summit, and the spiral band of sculptures with which the shaft is ornamented have their effect destroyed by the impossibility of seeing them in a horizontal line.   It must not, however, be forgotten that the column of Trajan was erected partly to show the vast labour expended in levelling the sides of the Quirinal and Capitoline for the construction of his Forum, and that it was enclosed within a narrow court, and did not rise much above the buildings which immediately surrounded it.[1]   It is not known whether in the case of the column of Marcus Aurelius any buildings were thus placed close round it.   The adjoining colonnades seem, as far as can be concluded from their remains, to have stood at some little distance.

Colossal columns were as genuine a creation of Imperial Rome as triumphal arches.   In the Republican era some of the statues in the Comitium stood upon columns ; but these were on a much smaller scale, and proportioned to the height of the statues themselves.   Some columnar monuments, as the columna rostrata of Duilius, were made to carry symbolic ornaments or trophies instead of statues.

---

[1] See the remarks in *R and C*. chap. vii. p. 146.   The pillar of Antoninus Pius was a monolith of red syenite.   See *R. and C.* chap. xiii. p. 333.

A column of Numidian marble was erected in honour of Julius Cæsar in the Forum;[1] and after his death honorary columns became very frequent in the Imperial age, not only at Rome, but in the provinces, as at Alexandria, Constantinople, Ancyra, and Cussy la Colonne, twelve miles from Beaune in Burgundy. They had the advantage, in an age of declining art, of concealing the defects of the statues erected at such a height above the eye; and when the Roman world afterwards became full of empty adulation, it was a cheap method of flattery to a patron to steal stones for a pedestal and a handsome column from the ruined temples, and erect them, with a fulsome inscription in his honour. Such is the column of Phocas in the Forum Romanum, a cento of fragments filched from some older buildings.[2]

Not more originality of design or elegance of taste is displayed in the decorations of the Roman tombs than in those of the triumphal arches and columns. The sarcophagus of Scipio Barbatus has been already noticed as an incongruous adaptation of Greek forms of ornamental work. Innumerable varieties of such adaptations might doubtless have been seen on all the principal roads leading out of Rome; but all these have now been stripped of their marble facings and reduced to mere cores of brick-

---

[1] See *R. and C.* chap. vi. p. 112.   [2] *Ibid.* chap. vi. p. 117.

work. We may gain some idea of the forms they generally assumed from the tombs at the Gate of Pompeii, which are mostly built in square or cubical stages, and present pediments, pilasters, and columns in different combinations. The tomb of Mamia at Pompeii, as restored by Mazois, is the miniature frontispiece of a Greek temple, with columns, entablature, and pediment complete.[1] Of this kind is also the tomb of Bibulus in the Via di Marforio at Rome, which has Doric pilasters and an Ionic entablature. Many tombs had a small peripteral or pseudo-peripteral cella mounted upon a cubical block. Such is the monument at S. Remy near Tarascon in France, which has a square base ornamented with bas-reliefs, and bearing a circular monopteral temple.

Egyptian forms were however sometimes employed, as in the pyramidal tombs of Cestius at the Porta S. Paolo, or Etruscan, as in the conical structure, commonly called the tomb of the Horatii and Curiatii near Albano. The bread-contractor's tomb, representing a pile of bread-baskets, which still stands at the outside of the Porta Maggiore, is an original but not a very pleasing design.[2]

---

[1] See Dyer's *Pompeii*, p. 530.

[2] See *R. and C.* chap. viii. 65, 197 ; Nibby, *Viaggio*, tom. ii. p. 143 ; *Monumenti dell' Inst.* 1837, plate xxxix. Compare with this strange device the tomb of Porsena figured in *Monumenti dell' Inst.* 1830. plate xiii. The cones probably represent the metæ of the circus. Hence the popular name of the Meta Sudans.

Foreign architectural forms, especially those of the Greek temple, were also reproduced in the rock-hewn tombs of the Romans. Few of these are to be found in the neighbourhood of Rome, as might be anticipated from the nature of the rocks. There are, however, some on the Flaminian road, and one very remarkable instance is to be seen in the garden of the monastery of Palazzola, on the edge of the Alban lake.[1] The rock-hewn tombs of Petra, once a much-frequented Roman station, present most extravagant instances of the Roman misapplication of columnar architecture. The façades of these tombs, exquisitely cut in rose-coloured sandstone, consist of a crowded medley of meaningless columns, half-columns, pilasters with curved or truncated entablatures, and pediments similar to those found in the Pantheon and in the still existing ruins of the eastern hemicycle of Trajan's Forum.

Far more characteristic of the Roman national taste in architecture are the huge cylindrical masses of stonework based upon square platforms, of which the mausolea of Augustus and Hadrian in Rome, and the tombs of Cæcilia Metella on the Appian Way and of Plautius on the bridge over the Anio at Tibur, are the most conspicuous examples. The ponderous walls of these massive

---

[1] Nibby, *Viaggio,* tom. ii. p. 125.

and indestructible marvels of masonry were essentially Roman ; but there the originality of their construction ends. We find, again, a strange combination of Orientalism with Hellenism in their outer decorative dress. The Mausoleum of Augustus was covered with terraces and trees in imitation of the Temple of Belus at Babylon, and the Mausoleum of Hadrian was dressed up with the usual shew array of pilasters, columns, and statues.[1]

Among the architectural decorations of Rome must also be reckoned the great colonnades of the Campus Martius[2] and the arcades of the fora and streets. The colonnades were built in the Greek fashion, with horizontal architraves of marble, and in some of them great magnificence was doubtless displayed. The arcades which were built by Nero along the principal streets were, on the contrary, constructed on piers, supporting arches and vaults of brickwork or concrete. They were specimens of the genuine Roman architecture in its unadorned simplicity and practical utility, for they served the double purpose of shelter from the sun and rain, and also of

---

[1] For the Mausoleum of Augustus, see *R. and C.* chap. xiii. pp. 343, 344 ; the Mausoleum of Hadrian, *R. and C.* chap. xi. p. 272. The planting of trees upon a sepulchral tumulus is mentioned in Homer. *Il.* vi. 419.

[2] See *R. and C.* chap. xiii. pp. 309, 316, 319, 331.

giving assistance in case of fire to the upper stories of the houses.

Not only imitation, but actual appropriation of the decorative works of Greece and other countries helped to adorn the streets and fora, the public buildings and arcades of Rome. The walls of their halls and temples were hung with the pictures of Zeuxis, Timanthus, Apelles, Aristides, and the other great masters of Grecian painting,[1] and filled with statues in bronze, ivory, and marble brought from Athens and Corinth.[2]   Of all the foreign architectural

---

[1] Plin. *N.H.* xxxv. § 60-150, gives a long account ; Rochette, *Peintures Antiques.*

[2] Preller, *Reg.* p. 231, gives from the Breviarium the following enumeration : twenty-two colossal equestrian statues, like that of Marcus Aurelius on the Capitol ; eighty gilt statues of gods, like that of the Capitoline Jupiter ; seventy-four ivory statues, like that of Minerva in the Forum of Augustus ; 3,785 bronze statues.   In the time of the Republic most of the statues stood in the Forum and Area Capitolina, but there were also collections in the Temple of Honour and Virtue, of Marcellus, in the colonnade of Metellus, and in the Atrium Libertatis of Asinius Pollio.   Augustus and Agrippa ornamented all the corners of the streets, the public fountains, the porticoes, parks, thermæ, and theatres with works of art.   At a later time the Forum Ulpium was filled with statues of celebrated personages ; and Alexander Severus is particularly mentioned as having taken great pains in the erection of such monuments.   Many of the great works of art were carried away to Constantinople ; but Cassiodorus speaks of a large number—especially of bronze statues—

ornaments collected in Rome, perhaps the most conspicuous were the Egyptian obelisks of syenite, which the emperors brought from the East and erected in the spinæ of the Circi. The Curiosum and Notitia mention only six of these, but the remains of eleven have been found at Rome.[1] In Egypt obelisks were always used in pairs, and erected at the entrance of the great temple portals, close to other gigantic monuments of nearly the same size and height. The two obelisks set in front of the great temple at Karnak overtopped the portico but little, and were in such a position suitably and naturally placed.[2] But the Romans, viewing them only as trophies of their vast Imperial dominion, cared but little to render them effective by placing them in appropriate situations. The Mausoleum of Augustus was indeed decorated in the true Egyptian style, with a pair of these monoliths at the portal, but in general they were not placed near anything of equal height, and presented nearly as forlorn

---

as still remaining in Theodoric's time. The final robbery was committed in the seventh century, when Constans II. carried the greater part of the Roman works of art to Constantinople.

[1] Zoega, *De Obeliscis*, cap. iv. Besides those at Rome, obelisks brought by the Romans have been found at Constantinople, Catana, Arelate, Velletri, and Benevento, and at Wansted, in England.

[2] See Reber, *Gesch. der Baukunst*, p. 167 ; Fergusson, *Arch.* vol. i. p. 108.

and naked an appearance as those in the modern squares of Rome.[1]

In proportion, however, as the architectural taste of the Romans deteriorated, their engineering skill seemed to grow. In the employment of the arch in great works of engineering skill, and in the development of its useful capabilities, the Romans have been the great teachers of the world. Neither the Assyrians nor the Egyptians, to whom the principle of the arch, both round and pointed, was well known, employed it except on a very moderate scale, and that chiefly in subterranean works.[2] Nor was the arch often used in any of the sacred buildings at Rome except in the interior. A superstitious dread of offending the deities by altering the form of their temples was quite sufficient to prevent any improvement in that department of architecture so long as Paganism lasted ; and even if this difficulty could have been got over, the Romans had no notion of making an arch ornamental as well as useful. But the increasing numbers of the Roman people, their gregarious habits, the necessity under the emperors for

---

[1] The mediæval name for obelisks was aguliæ (aculeus). Besides those mentioned in the Curiosum, there was one in the gardens of Sallust, another in the Circus of Maxentius, another in the Circus of Heliogabalus, and another in the Iseum and Serapeum in the Campus.   [2] See *R. and C.* p. xliv.

providing amusement and excitement on a large scale, and the pre-eminently practical genius of the race, soon produced their natural effects upon the national buildings. The Hellenic forms of public buildings, which sufficed for petty towns like Athens, or Corinth, or Ephesus, were totally inadequate to the conditions required in the metropolis of the world.

The population of Athens was probably less than 200,000,[1] while that of Rome was at least 1,000,000.[2] To afford room for the vast assemblies of people who would naturally meet in the public halls of so large a city the columnar structures of the Greeks were insufficient. Height, it was true, might have been obtained in their buildings by employing shafts of colossal dimensions; but then the difficulty of supporting the roof naturally arose. If the columns were placed so close together, as to allow the old short horizontal architraves of stone to be laid from the top of one capital to the next, a forest of great columns crowded together, such as the temple at Karnak contains, would have been the result ; and this would have ill suited the gregarious habits of the Romans.

---

[1] Böckh, *Economy*, chap. vii. p. 58.

[2] See Merivale, vol. iv. chap. xl. ; Dureau de la Malle in the *Mémoires de l'Académie des Inscr.* 1825.

The ancient plan of timber architraves and roofs was equally objectionable, for Rome had suffered so often and so much by fires that a natural dread would be felt of combustible materials.' And the Romans, even from the earliest times, as the massive structure of the Cloaca shows, despised all merely temporary and destructible work, and strove to combine the greatest possible utility and durability in their buildings.

From the determination to supply these needs arose the two great characteristic features of Roman architecture —the use of brickwork, and of the vaulted arch built of concrete. To carry a sufficient quantity of travertine for the whole mass of a large building from the distant quarries near Tibur was an expensive and laborious task ; and the tufa stone of the Roman hills was not only unpleasing in appearance. but soft, easily disintegrated by the weather, and unavailable for exterior walls. The Romans, therefore, had recourse to brickwork and masses of concrete, modes of building long before practised by the Etruscans, their earliest teachers in art,[1] and facilitated at Rome by the abundant beds of excellent clay to be found on the western bank of the Tiber, and by the un-rivalled mortar which could be made from the granular

---

[1] The walls of Arretium and Mevania were of brick, and some parts of those at Veii (Dennis, *Etruria*, vol. i. pp. 15, 16).

tufa (pozzolana) of their hills when mixed with lime. Roman brickwork and cement has become one of the marvels of the world. Even the damp and rotting climate of the Western Islands, where all stones decay, has not injured those well-known blocks of long, thin, flat bricks and stony concrete.

The earliest instance of the use of concrete (fartura) at Rome is in the ruins of the Emporium, B.C. 195. We find there a mass of concrete of rough stones mixed with mortar, and faced with reticulated work. The same mode of construction appears again in the Muro Torto,[1] at the corner of the Pincian hill, commonly said to be of the time of Sulla. An immense core of artificial concrete is there still remaining, as hard as a natural conglomerate rock. The improvements in the public walks have, unfortunately, of late years diminished this interesting mass of masonry considerably. The exterior surface is made of small pieces of tufa, with flat diamond-shaped faces, and wedge-shaped bases. These pointed bases were pressed into the concrete while it was still wet, so that the diagonals of their faces are horizontal and vertical, while the joints run in slanting lines. The name of opus reticulatum is commonly given to this kind of work.

---

[1] *R.* and *C.* chap. x. p. 260.

Sometimes the pieces of which the facing was made were irregularly placed, so as to present the appearance of polygonal masonry ; and this seems to have been preferred, in many cases, from the greater solidity of the joints when irregular. The appearance was not much considered, as such walls were frequently covered with stucco.

Many concrete walls were faced with regular courses of bricks instead of these bits of stone ; and in some we find the facing of opus reticulatum combined with courses of bricks, giving a sort of panel-work appearance to the wall ; and in other and later buildings, as the Circus of Maxentius, the brickwork is alternated with rough facings of brick-shaped tufa stones. The regular brickwork walls of the time of the early emperors are the most skilfully constructed.[1] The bricks used in them are flat like tiles, and the joints most carefully fitted with a thin layer of mortar. A more negligent style is found in the buildings of the Middle Empire ; the bricks became thicker, and the mortar less evenly and compactly laid.[2] It followed,

[1] Bunsen, *Beschreibung Roms*, vol. i. p. 189. The brickwork of the first century was the best. After the Antonine era it deteriorated.

[2] Ciampini on the different kinds of construction used at different epochs (Pelet, *L'Amphithéâtre de Nîmes*, p. 59) says : " I muri fatti a *pietre quadrate* dichiarono il tempo degli Etruschi, *l'incerto reticolato* il principio della Romana republica, il *certo reticolato* il fior della stessa, ed il *reticolato alternante con laterizio* il declinare della

naturally enough, when the great development of Roman building took place under the emperors, that conveniently situated beds of clay and brick-kilns became very desirable property, and that the excellences of various kinds of bricks were compared, and the bricks of certain kilns preferred. Partly from this reason, and partly in order to preserve a record of the date of a building, the larger bricks were stamped with the name of the proprietor of the kiln, and sometimes with the names of the consuls of the year. Large numbers of these stamps (bolli) have been collected and illustrated by the Roman anti- quaries.[1] The names found upon them include those of persons of high and even imperial rank, who owned kilns in the neighbourhood of Rome. The core and main body of the great Imperial buildings always con- sisted of concrete, with brick, or tufa, or marble facings ;

---

medesima : il *laterizio* i tempi d'Augusto et degli imperatori sequenti sino all' anno 200 dell' era volgare ; ed *il laterizio alternante a strati di tofo* i tempi di Gallieno e tutto il declinar dell' Impero ; selce, *croste di marmo, e mattoni* i tempi di Theodorico ; *il tumultuario aggregato a cemento* quei di Belisario ; i *quadrilateri bislunghi di tofo e mattoni* i giorni di Carlo Magno sino al 1,000, del qual epoca degenerò la construzione dei muri in opera tumultuaria e cemento e continua sino ai tempi presenti."

[1] See Becker and Marquardt, *Hdbh. Bd.* v. 1, p. 167. The figlinæ Domitianæ, Augustanæ, Caninianæ, Terentianæ, Fulvianæ, are among the most conspicuous.

and the famous boast of Augustus, that he found Rome
built of brick and left it built of marble, referred solely
to the outer casing of the public buildings with panel-
work of marble, the remains of the fastenings of which
may still be seen on some ruins in Rome.[1]

But even after the art of wall building had been
carried to the greatest perfection, there remained the
difficulties of roofing in the enormous spaces required
for the crowds who spent their lives in the public baths,
theatres, and amphitheatres of Rome. Greek architecture,
when carried out on a large scale, required enormous
blocks for the architraves, and for the far-projecting
cornice, such as we now see in the fragments of the
baths of Constantine in the Colonna Gardens at Rome,[2]
and in the temples of Baalbec and Palmyra. The
expense of labour and time required in cutting, carrying, raising, and laying such huge blocks was so
great, and the results so inadequate, that the practical
mechanical genius of the Romans soon discovered a
new method of roof-construction to meet the exigencies
of the case. The old semicircular stone arches were
found to be too heavy when constructed of the requisite

---

[1] As in those on the Palatine hill, and at the Baths of Caracalla,
and in the great basilicæ.   [2] See *R. and C.* p. 256.

span, and required enormously thick walls to support them. Recourse was therefore had to the lighter material of bricks, and the employment of these in vaulted arches removed the difficulty, and caused an entirely novel and fundamental change in the principles of the construction of roofs.[1] At the same time the arch was also introduced into wall building. The lightening of the roof made it possible to lessen the ponderous thickness of the supporting walls, and to relieve their monotonous flat surfaces with arched perforations. Even lighter materials than brick were occasionally employed. We find pumice stones, introduced in the vaulted arches of the Coliseum, Pantheon, and Thermæ of Caracalla;[2] and in the Circus of Maxentius and other ruins empty jars of pottery are to be seen built into the concrete vaulting to diminish the

---

[1] " It was the Romans with their tiles who first really understood the true employment of the arch."—Fergusson, *Arch.* i. p. 188.

[2] Hirt, *Gesch. der Bauk.* ii. p. 402 ; Winckelmann, *Obs. sur l'Arch.* vol. ii. pp. 554-556. The vaulted roofs of the Romans were made by simply piling a great thickness of concrete upon the centres and leaving it to consolidate. The concrete is $1\frac{1}{2}$ feet thick in some of the vaulted roofs of the thermæ at Rome. The cupola of the Church of S. Vitale, at Ravenna, is constructed of hollow pipes of pottery, and parts of the arches surrounding S. Stefano Rotondo at Rome are built in the same way. Fea, *Notes on Winckelmann,* loc. cit.

weight and to save materials. The vaulted arch, constructed with tiles as *voussoirs*, and concrete of great
thickness, ornamented with coffers of rich stucco work,
or with mosaic patterns, became, in the Imperial times,
the usual mode of construction in all buildings, from

BASILICA OF CONSTANTINE.

the ordinary rooms in houses to the vast halls of the
public edifices. The ruins on the Palatine hill, the great
Basilica of Constantine, and the Thermæ of Caracalla
and Diocletian still shew, in their huge vaults and masses

of concrete, the mechanical skill of the Roman architects. Three remaining arches of the Basilica of Constantine are sixty-eight feet in span, and eighty feet in height from the ground; and the vaulted concrete roof of the nave was eighty feet in span, and one hundred and fifteen feet in height.[1] They delighted in forming the most varied and novel combinations by crossing their vaults in different directions, by forming domes and semi-domes, and by introducing the concrete into every part of their buildings. The dome of the Pantheon shows at how early a period under Augustus they had carried the mechanical art of cupola building to the perfection of solidity and durability. With all their wonderful skill in brickwork, and in the construction of walls, arches, and vaulted roofs, there remained a stiffness and inflexibility in the forms they employed, which showed an inability to diverge from their received models. As in the mouldings of their decorative work they had confined themselves to arcs of the circle only, excluding the other curves employed by the Greeks, so in their arches they

---

[1] The roof of the Diribitorium was the largest in Rome, but it was constructed of wood. It was pulled down because it was not considered safe. Some of the beams were 100 feet in length. Flat roofs of timber cannot usually be made more than twenty-five feet wide with safety. Fergusson, *Arch.* vol. i. p. 158.

R

made use of the semicircle only, thus sacrificing variety to solidity. And while skill in engineering works and mechanical contrivance made rapid advances among them, the genius to imagine and power to adapt new ornamental additions in harmony with the new structural forms seemed to be entirely wanting. Unable quite to shake off their Greek fetters, they still sometimes covered up their arches with horizontal entablatures and pediments, and a mask of marble devices, in no way connected with the real parts of the building they concealed.

A prodigious display of constructive energy followed the adoption of the new features in their architecture. Not only Italy itself, but the provinces of the remotest west and east, were covered with huge engineering undertakings, in the shape of aqueducts, bridges, viaducts, amphitheatres, basilicas, and thermæ. Under Trajan and Hadrian the rage for building reached its height. The Ulpian Forum, for which a space was cleared between the Quirinal and Capitoline nearly equal to the area of the other three Imperial fora in Rome, was long one of the wonders of the world :

Verum cum ad Trajani forum venisset (Constantius) singularem sub omni caelo structuram, ut opinamur, etiam minimum adsensione mirabilem, haerebat attonitus, per giganteos contextus circumferens mentem, relatu ineffabiles, nec rursus mortalibus adpetendos (dixit.) --Amm. Marc. xvi. 10.

And the Villa of Hadrian, near Tibur, occupied the space of an ordinary Italian town, eight miles in circuit, and contained within itself a circus, three theatres, huge thermæ, an imitation of the Vale of Tempe, of Tartarus, and of the Elysian fields.[1] All these, to judge by the remains, were rather remarkable for their colossal size and for the imperial grandeur and force they expressed, than for their beauty of proportion or design. The Romans were in fact rather engineers than architects, and throughout their buildings they made elegance of appearance entirely subservient to practical utility.

Among the buildings appropriated to the public service at Rome, none were more important than the Basilicæ. Although their name is Greek,[2] yet they were essentially a Roman creation, and were used for practical purposes peculiarly Roman,—the administration of law, and the transaction of merchants' business. Historically, considerable interest attaches to them from their connection with the first Christian Churches. The name of Basilica was applied by the Romans equally to all large buildings intended for the

---

[1] See *R. and C.* chap. xiv.
[2] In Stat. *Silv.* i. 30, the Basilica of Paullus is called *regia*.

At laterum passus hinc Julia tecta tuentur
Illinc belligeri sublimis regia Paulli.

special needs of public business, and it does not appear
to have referred to the particular form in which such
buildings were arranged, so much as to the uses they
served. Generally, however, they took the form most
adapted to their purpose—a semicircular apse or tribunal
for legal trials, and a central nave, with arcades and
galleries on each side, for the transaction of business.
They existed not only as separate buildings, but also
as reception rooms attached to the great mansions
of Rome. The villa of the Gordian family on the Via
Prænestina contained three basilicas, each a hundred feet
long,[1] and a ground-plan of a basilica attached to the
Emperor's palace has lately been discovered upon the
Palatine hill.[2]

It is the opinion of some writers that these private
basilicæ, and not the public edifices, served as the model
for the Christian Basilica.[3] The first public basilicæ were
intended to serve as extensions of the fora, in which
shelter could be had from the weather, and interviews
carried on without interruption. The public men of
Rome, as well as the merchants, probably appeared in
them to afford opportunities for conversation on politics

[1] See *R. and C.* chap. xiv. p. 418.
[2] See *Cambridge Journal of Philology*, vol. ii. p. 84.
[3] *Zeitschrift für christlichen Archæologie;* Leipzic, 1859.

or business to those who wished to communicate news
to them or ask their advice.

Si interdum ad forum deducimur si uno basilicæ spatio hones-
tamur, diligenter observari videmur et coli.—Cic. *Pro Muræna*, 70.

Basilicarum loca adjuncta foris quam calidissimis partibus oportet
constitui, ut per hiemem sine molestia tempestatum se conferre in eas
negotiatores possint.—Vitruv. v. 1.

The convenience of a basilica therefore required that it
should be as spacious as a covered building could be
made, and should have, in connection with the central
area, some rooms for merchants' or notaries' offices.
Whether the primitive basilicæ at Rome borrowed their
ground-plan from the Greek stoa or not is a disputed
question. The Stoa of the Hellanodicæ at Elis, described
by Pausanias as consisting of three parallel naves divided
by columns, seems to present the model upon which most
of the great basilicæ at Rome were planned, but the
description is so brief as to leave us in doubt.

The Æmilian Basilica in the Forum Romanum is the
first of which we have any structural knowledge. A
fragment of the Capitoline map, which is supposed to
give the ground-plan of this building, shews it as divided
into several naves by rows of columns. The plan of the
Basilica Julia has been discovered by excavations carried
on during the last ten years, and shews us a central
rectangular nave with a double arcaded corridor on all

the four sides. There is no trace of columns having been used, but the arcades were supported by solid piers of masonry with pilasters, and resembled the arcades underneath the seats of the Coliseum. Nor was there any apse in the Julian Basilica, a part which is usually considered characteristic of this class of building.

Vitruvius gives a description of a basilica built by himself at Fanum (Fano) in Umbria. In this building one of the longer sides formed the front facing the forum, as in the Basilica Julia, but it differed in having a semicircular tribunal on the other longer side, with a Temple of Augustus attached to it. From Vitruvius's description it appears that the Roman architects allowed themselves great freedom as to the arrangements of their buildings, and did not by any means rigidly adhere to one type.

The basilica at Pompeii is an oblong, with one of the shorter sides turned towards the forum, and has in front a chalcidium or portico. There is no apse, but a raised square platform served as the tribunal. In the great Ulpian Basilica there were four naves divided by rows of columns, and two tribunals, or semicircular apses, in the shorter sides of the oblong.[1]

---

[1] See *R. and C.* chap. vii. p. 144, and plan of the Fora of the Emperors.

Other differences of form are to be found in the ancient Italian basilicæ,[1] which shew that the shape of such buildings depended upon the space to be occupied and upon the taste of the architect, and was not regulated by any strict rules of construction. None of them were, it is probable, very ornamental buildings, and certainly that one of which we have the most relics left, the great Basilica of Constantine, was rather a stupendous exhibition of mechanical skill than a building with any pretence to beauty of form. The interior was, it is true, ornamented with colossal columns and marble sculpture, and the monotony of the huge vaulted roof relieved by coffers and rosettes, but the exterior was very ungainly and heavy in appearance. We find in it three naves, the central one higher than the rest, and so arranged that, whether the building was entered from the side next the Sacra Via or from that next to the Temple of Venus and Rome, it presented a triple division of the interior, with an apse at the end of each central division opposite to the entrance.[2] It is perhaps due to the protection of the massive arches of the roof (which at the present day support a large kitchen garden) that

---

[1] In the basilicas at Præneste and Aquinum there is a single nave only. Hirt, *Gesch. der Baukunst*, ii. p. 222. See *R. and C.* chap. xiv.

[2] See *R. and C.* chap. viii. p. 166.

this basilica has so long survived its contemporaries, most of which had timbered roofs, and were therefore liable to destruction by fire.

Several buildings were erected by the Emperors for the purpose of preserving the large collections of manuscripts. The Library of Asinius Pollio was the first public library at Rome, but we know nothing of its size or architectural arrangements.[1] The famous Palatine Library of Augustus seems to have been connected with the Temple of the Palatine Apollo by a colonnade, and was itself a large hall capable of containing a colossal statue of Apollo. Whether the poetical descriptions of Propertius and Ovid apply to the library building itself, or to the Temple of Apollo, or to the colonnades attached to them, is not certain.[2]

We know more about the plan of the Library of Trajan, which formed a part of the group of buildings surrounding his forum. One side of it is represented on the Capitoline map as a rectangular building, standing to the north of the eastern tribune. The interior has a row of columns

---

[1] See Preller, *Reg.* p. 219. Twenty-eight libraries are catalogued by the Regionaries and Mirabilia.

[2] A recitation-room was at a later period attached to the Palatine Library. Perhaps the lecture-room lately excavated may have been the place to which Pliny alludes. *Cambridge Philolog. Journal*, vol. ii. p. 87.

running round it, and it is flanked by the columns of the basilica on one side, and by those of the Temple of Hadrian on the other. There was a corresponding building on the other side of the small square court in which the pillar stood; and in one of these was the Greek, and in the other the Latin library. This mode of division into two departments, connected by an atrium ornamented with the busts and statues of famous literary men, seems to have been the usual form of Roman public libraries.[1] The library at the Porticus Octaviæ was probably a double building.[2]

The facilities for public traffic between the different parts of Rome were long neglected, and the streets having been rebuilt, after the Gallic conflagration, without a regular plan, must have been crooked and inconvenient. But as soon as the nation found itself in possession of funds available for works of public utility, the streets, roads, and bridges were taken in hand, and methods of construction adopted, the solidity and massive strength of which was as unrivalled as that of the Roman masonry.[3]

---

[1] See *R. and C.* chap. vii. p. 146, and the Plan of the Forum Trajani. Preller, *Reg.* p. 220.

[2] See *R. and C.* chap. xiii. p. 310.

[3] Strabo, v. p. 235. Tolls were taken on paved roads for repairs. *Bull. d'Inst.* 1845, p. 132; 1847, p. 174.

An examination of the existing Roman roads has shown that they were constructed exactly according to the rules laid down by Vitruvius for the pavement of floors ; [1] and this is further confirmed by a passage of Statius, describing the reconstruction of a part of the Appian road by Domitian. " If the pavement is to be laid," says Vitruvius, " on the ground-floor, it must first be ascertained whether the earth is thoroughly solid ; and if it is, it should be levelled, and the first and second beds (statumen and rudus) laid down : [2] if, however, the whole or a part of the earth be unsound, it must be very carefully hardened by ramming with beetles. Then let the lowest bed be laid (statuminetur) with stones not larger than will fill the hand. When this is done, the second bed may be laid (ruderetur) with rubble (rudus). If the rubble be new, it must be mixed with a fourth part of lime ; if it has been used before, with two parts of lime to five. The rubble must then be rammed down very hard with wooden beetles, by gangs of ten men, till the thickness is not more than nine inches. Above

---

[1] Nibby, *Dissert. delle Vie degli Antichi.*

[2] *Statumen* is used in the sense of "foundation." *Rudus* is defined by Isodorus to be " lapides contusi et calce admixti," broken pebbles mixed with lime. *Nucleus*, the kernel, as being inclosed and protected by the other beds.

the rubble bed must be laid the kernel of the pavement (nucleus), composed of potsherds mixed with a third part of lime. The thickness of this should not be less than six fingers' breadth. The paving stones must be bedded in the kernel, and accurately adjusted with a level." [1]   The stone used in the streets of Rome for paving was either the hard black basaltic lava obtained in many places near Rome, particularly in the quarries near the tomb of Cæcilia Metella, and at Bovillæ on the Appian road, and also on the Via Labicana, or the travertine from Tibur, or peperino from Gabii. The first, which has a conchoidal cleavage, was laid in polygonal blocks, fitted accurately together, as we see in the fragments of the old roads still visible on the Appian, Latin, and Tiburtine roads. The two others were laid in rectangular blocks, such as may be seen in the pavement of Trajan's Forum, and the part of the Forum Romanum, near the column of Phocas. The former method was called "silice sternere," the latter "saxo

---

[1] The width of the principal Roman road, the Via Appia, is fifteen feet. The Via Tusculana is only eleven feet wide, and the cross roads in the Campagna are not more than nine feet wide. There is a roadway (*viottolo*) paved with basalt, branching out from the Via Appia under the tomb of Cæcilia Metella, towards the Circus of Maxentius, which is only four feet wide. Nibby, *Diss. delle Vie degli Antichi*, p. 38, in Nardini, *Roma Antica*, tom. iv.

quadrato sternere," and the road so paved was called
"stratæ."

It must not be supposed that all Roman streets or
roads were laid down in this elaborate manner. There
were two other kinds of roads mentioned by Ulpian,
the gravelled road (glareata), and the earthen road simply
levelled and left without further covering (terrena). In
early times, as in the censorship of Fulvius (B.C. 174),
only the streets within the city were paved with lava,
and the roads outside the walls laid with gravel ; but
afterwards, so far as can be ascertained, all the consular
roads were paved with stone.[1]

> Nec taceat monimenta viae, quem Tuscula tellus
>   Candidaque antiquo detinet Alba Lare.
> Namque opibus congesta tuis hic glarea dura
>   Sternitur, hic apta jungitur arte silex.—Tibull. i. 7, 57.

In places where the road passed over rock, the statumen
and rudus were dispensed with, and the nucleus and
pavement only laid, as on the Appian road near Albano.
Besides the central causeway, a Roman road had, in
general, a raised footway on each side,[2] about four
inches high, edged either with slabs of basaltic lava

---

[1] Nibby, *Diss. delle Vie degli Antichi*, p. 39.
[2] Crepido, margo, umbo.

or squared stones. Nibby mentions a piece of road
which still shows footways of this kind, leading from
the Labican into the Latin road, about two miles from
Tusculum. The centre of the footway was composed
of gravel, and some of the kerbstones were longer than
others, and were driven into the mass of gravel so as to
bind the margin of the pathway firmly into it.[1]

When a road was carried along the side of a hill, or
across a valley, although the Roman architects did not
build such viaducts as are now constructed for railways,
yet they took great pains to modify the slopes of the
hills as much as possible, by massive substructions of
masonry, or by cutting away the rocks, or even tunnelling
through them. In the valley of Ariccia, between Albano
and Genzano, the massive substructions of the old Appian
road still remain ; on the Via Prænestina the Ponte di
Nono carries the road over seven massive arches formed
by blocks of peperino and tufa, fitted together without
mortar, and of the most solid construction possible ;[2]
and on the way from Rocca di Papa to the old Via
Latina, near the so-called Camp of Hannibal, Nibby

---

[1] Hence these longer kerbstones are called *gomphi* by Statius.

Tunc umbonibus hinc et hinc coactis,
Et crebris iter alligare gomphis.—*Sylvae*, iv. 3, 47.

[2] *Westphal. Campagna*, p. 98.　*Old Rome*, p. 221.

found a cutting made in the side of Mount Algidus, fifty feet in depth, for the passage of a cross road from the Via Latina to the Via Triumphalis or Albana.[1]

The tunnel on the road from Puteoli to Naples, 2,244 feet in length and twenty-one in width, mentioned by Strabo[2] as the work of Cocceius in the time of Tiberius, is well known to travellers; and the cutting and tunnel of the Furlo pass, on the Flaminian road, through the Monte d'Asdrubale near Fanum, in the valley of the Metaurus, still bears an ancient inscription, stating that it was the work of the Emperor Vespasian. Claudian has described this pass, in his poem on the sixth consulate of Honorius, as one of the sights to be noticed by Honorius on his road from Ravenna to Rome.

> Qua mons arte patens vivo se perforat arcu
> Admittitque viam sectae per viscera rupis.[3]
>
> Claud. vi. *Cons. Honor.* 500.

---

[1] Nibby, *op. cit.* p. 42.

[2] Strabo, bk. v. p. 243. Seneca calls it Crypta Neapolitana, and complains of having been well-nigh stifled with the dust in it, which shews that it was not then paved with Vesuvian lava, as it now is:

A ceromate (wrestlers' ointment) nos haphe (wrestlers' white sand) excepit in crypta Neapolitana.—Sen. *Ep.* 57, 1.

[3] Where Art takes a road through a mountain, which is penetrated by an arch, and you can make your way through the bowels of the rocks.

Of a similar kind, but for a different purpose, were the great cutting and tunnelling works undertaken for the regulation of the water of the smaller Italian lakes. The Veline lake, near Reate, on the banks of which Cicero's friend Axius lived,

Rosea rura Velini.—*Æn.* vii. 712.

Quod lacus Velinus a M' Curio emissus interciso monte in Narem defluit, ex quo est illa siccata et humida tamen modice Rosea.—Cic. *Ad Att.* iv. 15.

was drained by M. Curius Dentatus in B.C. 290, by means of a deep cutting, through which the now celebrated cascade of Terni falls. The tunnel of the Alban lake, made in B.C. 395, is also still in activity, and draws off the superfluous water.

Romane aquam Albanam cave lacu contineri, cave in mare manare suo flumine sinas.—Liv. v. 16.

This tunnel cut through the grey peperino of the side of the lake, which lies in a crater-like hollow under the Alban hill, is 7,500 feet in length, 5 feet wide, and 7 or 8 feet in height. At several places the vertical shafts by which the chips of rock were removed, and also the sloping approaches for the entrance of the workmen, can be traced. At the end where the water flows from the lake there is careful provision made, by the position of the

walls, for resisting too sudden a flow of water, and also by
a piscina limaria for the deposit of mud and refuse. At
the other end, where the water issues from the tunnel, is a
large reservoir, whence the water was distributed in different
directions for irrigation.[1] The principle of the arch was
evidently known to those who made this tunnel, and it is
probable that it was bored under the direction of Greek
engineers sent in consequence of the Delphic oracular
response which ordered the work to be undertaken. At
all events, the Greeks, from the formation of their own
hills and lakes, were well acquainted with this kind of
tunnel-work.

But perhaps the most difficult undertaking of the kind
that Roman energy ever carried out was the tunnel of the
Fucine lake, made by Claudius in order to reclaim the
neighbouring district from the water.

> Te nemus Anguitiae vitrea te Fucinus unda
> Te liquidi flevere lacus.—*Æn.* vii. 759.

This is a far longer tunnel than the Alban, being nearly
three English miles in length, nineteen feet high, and nine
feet in width. It was cut through the hard limestone rock
of Monte Salviano, which rises 1,000 feet above the level

---

[1] See *R. and C.* chap. xiv. p. 357.

of the lake, and gave the water of the lake an outlet into the Liris.[1]

Inter maxime memoranda equidem duxerim . . . . . montem perfossum ad lacum Fucinum emittendum.—Plin. *N.H.* xxxvi. 124.

To the same class as these tunnels belonged also the great cloacæ of Rome, which not only served as outlets to carry off the superfluous rain-water and sewage of the city, but also to drain off the enormous quantity of water daily poured into Rome by the aqueducts, which must have increased the volume of the Tiber to an appreciable degree.[2]

Vos mihi quae Latium septenaque culmina nymphae
Incolitis Tibrimque novis attollitis undis.[3]

Stat. *Silv*. i. 5. 24.

Some of these great archways, no doubt, lie buried under the rubbish of modern Rome. The only two large

---

[1] Fabretti's treatise, *De Emissario Fucini*, is most complete : Rome, 1683. Kramer, *Fuciner ins. See :* Berlin, 1839.

[2] In Frontinus' time the *nine* aqueducts supplied 15,000 quinariæ or pipes, an inch and a quarter in diameter. The three aqueducts now remaining, the Aqua Vergine (Virgo), the Aqua Paola (Aurelia), and the Felice (Claudia), pour 20,485,100 cubic feet of water into Rome daily. In the time of Procopius there were fourteen aqueducts.

[3] You must tell me, you Nymphs who go through Latium to the seven hills, and raise the level of the Tiber with fresh waters. (*R. and C.* pp. 11, 24.)

cloacæ now known and still utilised are the Cloaca Maxima and the cloaca which leads from the Pantheon to the Tiber.

Great engineering works in connection with the harbours of Italy and the mouths of the great rivers of the Mediterranean were also undertaken by the Romans. They laboured under the serious disadvantage of having no large harbours on the west coast of Italy. The first great effort to remedy this was made in the time of Augustus by Agrippa, who made a canal from the Gulf of Baiæ to the two lakes of Lucrinus and Avernus.[1]

> An memorem portus Lucrinoque addita claustra
> Atque indignatum magnis stridoribus aequor
> Julia·qua ponto longe sonat unda refuso
> Tyrrhenusque fretis immittitur aestus Avernis.
> Virg. Georg. ii. 161.
> Debemur morti nos nostraque, sive receptus
> Terra Neptunus classes aquilonibus arcet,
> Regis opus.—Hor. Ars Poet. 63.

This was considered one of the great marvels of the age at the time, but it does not seem to have long continued to be the station of the Roman fleet, which was removed to Misenum.

Classem Miseni et alteram Ravennæ ad tutelam Superi et Inferi maris conlocavit. (Augustus).—Suet. Oct. 49.

---

[1] See R. and C. chap. xii. pp. 279-286.

A great reservoir, called Piscina Mirabile, and extensive subterranean warehouses (cento camarelle), were built there for the service of the fleet.

Great harbours were constructed at a later time, by Claudius at Ostia, and by Trajan at Centum Cellæ. The extent and cost of Claudius's operations may be inferred from the fact that he sank the great ship upon which Caligula brought a huge obelisk from Alexandria, to assist in forming a foundation for his breakwater.[1]

Mole objecta quam quo stabilius fundaret navem ante demersit, qua magnus obeliscus ex Aegypto fuerat advectus.—Suet. *Claud.* 20.

(Navem) perductam Ostiam portus gratia mersit.—Plin. *N. H.* xxxvi. 70.

Trajan's breakwater at Centum Cellæ, forty-seven miles from Rome, was formed of a mass of huge stones, sunk in the sea, and had a lighthouse at each end.

Habebit hic portus et jam habet nomen auctoris eritque vel maxime salutaris. Nam per longissimum spatium litus inportuosum hoc receptaculo utetur.—Plin. *Ep.* vi. 31, 17.

It was of course natural that bridges should be among the first buildings to which the Roman engineers would apply the principle of the arch. The bridges over the Tiber at Rome are described in most works on Rome,[2]

---

[1] See *R. and C.* chap. xiv.　　[2] *Ibid.* chap. xi.

and therefore need not further be alluded to here than to remark that, after the piers of the Æmilian bridge—the oldest stone bridge at Rome—were built, the completion of the arches, perhaps from the old prejudice against permanent bridges, was not carried out till thirty-seven years afterwards.[1] This seems to shew that the construction of bridges of stone was then a matter about which some hesitation was felt.[2]

The medal figured by Nardini, which gives an outline of the Ælian bridge at Rome, shews the mode in which the Romans endeavoured to decorate their bridges.[3] A row of pedestals, rising from the parapets of the bridge, support statues, and the parapets are built with an open balustrade instead of a solid wall. In general, however, the Roman bridges were left without ornament ; and I am not aware that attempts were often made to dress them with Greek decorative forms. The bridge of Rimini, built by Tiberius, and entirely composed of marble, has decorated pediments and columns upon the piers, showing that, at the time of its construction, Greek decorations were still considered

---

[1] The finest ancient Roman bridges are at Rimini (see Eustace, *Classical Tour*, vol. i. p. 279 ; Orelli, *Inscr.* 604) and at Alcantara in Spain (Gruter, *Inscr.* p. 162).

[2] The Fabrician bridge was not constructed till 62 B.C.: *R. and C.* chap. xi. p. 265. [3] Nardini, *Roma Antica*, vol. iii. tav. ii. No. 57.

necessary adjuncts of any considerable building. Trajan was the great Roman bridge builder, and in his forum the worst faults of the Roman adaptations of Greek art were illustrated ;[1] yet no such affectation extended to the great engineering works of that emperor. His bridge over the Tagus, at Norba Cæsariana (Alcantara), is perfectly plain and unadorned, yet produces, by a peculiar arrangement of the arches, which are sprung from different levels, a singular impression of graceful proportion united with compact and durable strength.[2] The bridge of Apollodorus over the Danube, represented in the sculptures of Trajan's column, and described by Dion Cassius, was a great effort of engineering genius ; but as the piers only were of stone, and the upper part of woodwork, scarcely any remains of it are now visible.[3]

The want of a supply of water at a high level first led the Roman architects to raise their aqueducts on the mighty ranges of arches which now form the most striking feature of the Roman Campagna. The most ancient aqueduct, the Appia, constructed in B.C. 312, was entirely subterranean ; and even the Aqua Virgo, the sixth in chronological order of the fourteen which flowed into

---

[1] See *R. and C.* chap. vii. p. 143.

[2] Figured in Fergusson's *Architecture*, vol. i. p. 346.

[3] See *R. and C.* chap. vii. p. 150.

Rome in the time of Procopius,[1] is chiefly subterranean
But the Claudian aqueduct, begun by Caligula and
finished by Claudius, and the Anio Novus were at a height
sufficient to supply the top of the highest hills at Rome,
and were carried upon lofty arches during a great part of
their course.

Quippe a xxxx lapide ad eam excelsitatem ut omnes urbis montes
lavarentur influxere Curtius atque caeruleus fontes et Anien novos :
erogatum in id opus H S oo oo oo D.—Plin. *N. H.* xxxvi. 15, 122.

Marsasque nives et frigora ducens
Marcia, praecelsis quarum vaga molibus unda
Crescit, et innumero pendens transmittitur arcu.

Stat. *Silv.* i. 5, 26.

For ten miles out of the whole forty-six traversed by the
Aqua Claudia it is supported on arches ; and the Anio
Novus flowed for fourteen miles on the summit of an
arched aqueduct, some of the arches of which were 109
feet in height.[2]

Altissimus est Anio novus, proxima Claudia, tertium locum tenet
Julia, quartum Tessula, dehinc Marcia.—Frontinus, *De Aquaed.*
14, 15, 18.

The arches of the Marcian aqueduct, first constructed in

---

[1] See Bunsen, *Beschreibung*, Bd. i. p. 195.

[2] Pipes to bring water from the sources of the Marcia near Subiaco
are now laid by a Roman water company.

B.C. 145, are not nearly so high as those of the Claudian, but are even more solid and durable. At the Porta Furba, an arch constructed by Sixtus V. for the Aqua Felice, about three miles from the Porta S. Giovanni on the Via Tusculana, the ruins of these aqueducts are best seen. The Aqua Marcia and the Aqua Claudia there run nearly in parallel lines on the left-hand side of the Frascati road, which they cross at the Porta Furba. The former is carried on massive arches at a level twenty-five feet lower than the former.

Aeternum Marcius humor opus.—Prop. iv. 22, 24.

Various kinds of stone are used in these arcades, but chiefly travertine and peperino. In the branch of the Aqua Claudia built by Nero to supply the Palatine and Cælian hills, which diverges from the main aqueduct at the Porta Maggiore, the arches are of the best Roman brick-work ;[1] and the aqueduct of Alexander Severus,[2] a great number of the arches of which are to be seen on the left of the Via Labicana, near Torre di Cento Celle, was also built of brick. As the Romans used pipes for the distribution of the water in the city itself, no other

---

[1] See Winckelmann, œuvres, vol. ii. p. 546.
[2] This aqueduct supplied the thermæ in the Campus Martius. See *R. and C.* chap. xiii. p. 341.

explanation of the reason why all these lofty arches were built for a purpose which could have been equally served by subterranean pipes is satisfactory, except that of Fabretti, who remarks, in noticing the strange course of the Aqua Alexandrina, that a reason may be found for this apparent waste of labour in the magnificent appearance of such structures as these aqueducts, the arches of which are frequently not less than seventy feet in height.[1]

> Quid loquor aeria pendentes fornice rivos,
> Qua vix imbriferas tolleret iris aquas?
>
> Rutilius Num. 1, 97.

The popularity gained by affording so much employment, and the need of work for the host of slaves must also be reckoned. The arches are often taken across a valley in preference to an obviously shorter and more level course, apparently for the sole purpose of carrying an archway across which might be conspicuous.

---

[1] Fabretti, *De Aquæd.*, Rome, 1788, p. 11. It appears from Vitruv. lib. viii. chap. 7, that Roman aqueducts were sometimes made with leaden or earthen pipes. Ductus autem aquae fiunt generibus tribus, rivis per canales structiles, aut fistulis plumbeis, seu tubulis fictilibus. —Vitruv. viii. 7, 1 (6), 1. Pliny, xxxi. § 57, recognises the principle that water will find its level in a pipe. Quam (aquam) surgere in sublime opus fuerit plumbo veniat; subit altitudinem exortus sui.— Plin. *N. H.* xxxi. 6, § 57.

The same fondness for display led the emperors, at the places where the line of their aqueducts crossed the public roads leading out of Rome, to erect a secondary kind of triumphal arch, upon which an inscription might be placed, recording the name and titles of the builder and of the successive restorers of the aqueducts.[1] At the Porta Maggiore and the Porta S. Lorenzo specimens of these commemorative archways are to be seen,[2] and above them the specus, or the channel in which the water flowed was placed. These channels are about three or four feet wide and seven or eight feet high, so as to allow a man easily to walk along them for the purpose of clearing away the sediment which rapidly accumulated. The whole breadth of the arcade was generally from ten to twelve feet. At intervals along the specus were vent holes large enough to admit a man's body, and at the sources of the aqueduct and also at certain distances along its course were basins (piscinæ limariæ) in which the earthy deposit was allowed to settle. There were, besides these piscinæ, considerable reservoirs (castella)

---

[1] The Pont du Gard near Nismes is the best extant specimen of the grandeur and simplicity of Roman buildings when unadorned by Greek columns and pilasters. See Clerisseau, *Antiquités de la France,* p. 127.

[2] See woodcuts in *R. and C.* chap. v. pp. 63, 65.

here and there, to keep stores of water either for irrigation or for any sudden emergency. The reservoir called the Sette Sale at Rome, on the Esquiline,[1] is still well preserved ; and a more remarkable building of the kind is to be seen at Misenum, where a supply of water was kept for the Roman fleet stationed there.

The aqueducts supplied many ornamental cisterns and fountains in Rome. The cisterns and wells were frequently surrounded with a circular marble edging decorated with bas-reliefs, specimens of which may be seen in the Roman museums, or they were protected by a round monopteral building with a cupola.[2]

The only ruined fountain which now remains *in situ* at Rome is the Meta Sudans ;[3] and not a trace is left of its marble casing, which was probably very splendid. But the museums of Rome contain numerous stone basins of porphyry, granite, basalt, alabaster, marble, and breccia, which show the amount of cost and labour expended on such ornamental works. A beautiful little house fountain is preserved in the Capitoline Museum, formed in the shape of a tripod, in the centre of which a hollow column

---

[1] *R. and C.* chap. ix. p. 232.

[2] See Preller, *Regionen*, p. 108, who gives a number of interesting details about the lacus and nymphæa of Rome.

R. and C. chap. viii. pp. 170, 237.

throws up a jet of water, which, falling into the basin, is carried away through the legs of the tripod.[1]

Other large public fountains were made in the shape of cascades, like the modern Fontana Trevi. The ruins of one of these, called "The Trophies of Marius," were preserved on the Esquiline. The front of this consisted of two raised ledges, upon which the water flowed from the reservoir behind by six or seven openings, and fell into a basin. The upper part was ornamented with a large niche for sculpture in the centre, and two arched openings at the sides, in which the so-called trophies of Marius, now placed on the ascent to the Capitol, stood.[2]

The castella of the aqueducts were also frequently rendered ornamental by marble decorations and statues. Pliny tells us that Agrippa alone, when Ædile, constructed at Rome no less than "seven hundred cisterns, fifty jets of water, and one hundred and thirty castella, which he decorated with three hundred marble and bronze statues, and four hundred marble columns."

---

[1] See Jordan in *Ann. dell' Inst.* 1867, p. 398. M. Jordan conjectures that the stars engraved on the Pianta Capitolina represent putealia and fountains. There is one in the guard-house of the Vigiles, lately excavated, of this star shape. See Bellori's " Pianta," cap. ix. 5, in *Græv. Thes.* Several beautiful house fountains are preserved at Pompeii. See Dyer's *Pompeii*, pp. 87-90, 385.

[2] See *R. and C.* chap. ix. p. 227.

Besides the Castra Prætoriana,[1] which were built by Tiberius, some other permanent camps in Rome deserve a passing notice among the principal public buildings. These were the Castra Peregrina on the Cælian, the Castra

PORTA FURBA.

Ravennatium in the Trastevere, the Castra Misenatium, and the Castra Priora and Nova of the Equites Singularii. Architecturally, they were probably less ornamental even

---

[1] See *R. and C.* chap. v. p. 61.

than the Castra Prætoriana, but must have been spacious and conspicuous buildings, and contributed to the general impression produced by the aspect of Rome. The Peregrini were foreign troops, possibly introduced as a counterpoise to the Prætorian Guards by Septimius Severus, who boasted that he had quadrupled the number of troops in Rome ;[1]

Τῆς τε ἐν Ῥώμῃ δυνάμεως αὐτῆς τετραπλασιασθείσης.—Herodian, iii. 13 ;

and the Misenates and Ravennates were detachments of the marines from Misenum and Ravenna, who were employed in the amphitheatre to manage the velaria.

A militibus classiariis qui vela ducebant in amphitheatro interimi. —*Hist. Aug. Com.* 15.

The Equites Singularii seem to have been a picked body of cavalry attached to the Emperor's body-guard, who were used as couriers to carry despatches.[2]

Accessit ala singularium.—Tac. *Hist.* iv. 70.

Augustus, among the other great services he rendered to the city, built large public warehouses, mills, wash-houses, and bake - houses, which were improved and

---

[1] Preller, *Regionen*, p. 99.

[2] *Ibid.* p. 99 ; *Notitia Dign.*, ed. Böcking, p. 788 ; *Ann. dell' Inst.* 1850.

enlarged by subsequent emperors, until they became
sufficiently important to be included in the catalogues
of public buildings given by the writers of the *Notitia*
and *Curiosum*. Among the warehouses were the papyrus
warehouse, near the booksellers' quarter in the Vicus
Sandaliarius, at the back of the Templum Pacis ; the
pepper and spice warehouse in the same neighbourhood ;
the warehouses of Agrippa and Germanicus, near the
shops of the Vicus Tuscus ; and those named after Galba
and Anicius near the Emporium.

The Capitoline map gives a plan of one of these buildings, the Horrea Lolliana, which exhibits it as a large
central hall, with open arcades in rows on each side.
They were built of stone in order to be fireproof, and
Nero was obliged, on account of their solidity and strength
of construction, to employ military engines in pulling
some of them down when he wished to extend his Golden
House over their site.[1]

Et quaedam horrea circum domum Auream, quorum spatium
maxime desiderabat, ut bellicis machinis labefacta atque inflammata
sint quod saxeo muro constructa erant.—Suet. *Nero*, 38.

Pliny states that public bakehouses were unknown in
Rome before the year of the city 586, but in the Imperial

---

[1] See Preller, *Regionen*, p. 102.

times the contractors for bread became important persons, as may be seen from the monument of Eurysaces at the Porta Maggiore, and from the mention of a Collegium Pistorum at Rome in the reign of Trajan.[1]

Et annonae perpetuae mire consultum reperto firmatoque pistorum collegio.—Aur. Vict. *Caes.* xiii. 5.

The pistrina publica are enumerated in the catalogues of the Regionarii, together with the horrea and balnea, and were therefore probably buildings of considerable size and prominence.

With all their earnestness and practical sagacity in public business and in works of national utility, the Romans, or perhaps it should rather be said the motley crowd who in Imperial times inhabited the city of Rome, were a people passionately fond of recreation and excitement. The buildings raised for these purposes were the most magnificent and durable in the empire. While the temples of the gods and the fora of the emperors have nearly disappeared, the thermæ and amphitheatres still defy the inroads of time, and, if spared by the hands of man, seem likely to justify the epithet of Eternal applied so frequently to Rome.

The Roman thermæ were a combination on a huge

---

[1] See Preller, *Regionen*, p. 111. See *R. and C.* chap. v. p. 65.

scale of the common balneæ with the Greek gymnasia.[1]
Their usual form was that of a large quadrangular space,
the sides of which were formed by various porticoes,
exedræ, and even theatres for gymnastic and literary
exercises, and in the centre of which stood a block of
buildings containing the bath rooms and spacious halls
for undergoing the complicated process of the Roman
warm bath.

Lavacra in modum provinciarum exstructa.—Amm. Marc. xvi. 10.

The area covered by the whole group of buildings was,
in many cases, very large. The court of the Baths of
Caracalla inclosed a space of 1,150 feet on each side, with
curvilinear projections on two sides. The central mass
of building was a rectangle, 730 feet by 380, covering an
area equal to that occupied by the English Houses of
Parliament together with Westminster Hall ; and the
largest hall, which St. George's Hall at Liverpool resembles very much, was 170 feet in length, 82 feet in

---

[1] The older thermæ are sometimes called "gymnasia":—

Dedicatisque thermis atque gymnasio senatui quoque et equiti oleum
præbuit.—Suet. *Ner.* 12.

Gymnasium eo anno dedicatum a Nerone praebitumque oleum
equiti ac senatui Graeca facilitate.—Tac. *Ann.* xiv. 47.

Λακωνικὸν γὰρ τὸ γυμνάσιον . . . . ἐπεκάλεσε. He called his gymnasium
(Thermae) a Laconicum.—Dion Cass. liii. 27.

width, and 120 feet in height.[1] It was roofed by inter-
secting vaults of brickwork in three compartments supported by eight huge columns, similar to those now
standing in the Thermæ of Diocletian[2] (Sta. Maria degli
Angeli).   The other great Imperial thermæ of Rome,
those of Nero, Titus, Domitian, Diocletian, and Constantine, were probably upon the same plan as the Thermæ
Caracallæ.   All were built of brick, and the interior was
decorated with stucco, mosaics, or slabs of marble, and
other ornamental stones.   These architectural embellish-
ments have in all cases disappeared, with the exception
of the grand granite columns of the great hall of Diocletian's Thermæ, and it is therefore impossible to say
what was the original appearance they presented.   Some
idea of the effect produced by their stuccoed roofs may
be gained from the coffers in the roof of the Basilica of
Constantine, or the Temple of Venus and Rome, or the
interior of the Pantheon.[3]   It is not likely that the taste
displayed in the ornamental work would be faultless,
since most probably the vulgar love of the Romans for
costly splendour shewed itself in an exaggerated form
in these halls of luxurious recreation ; but the whole im-

---

[1] *R. and C.* chap. ix. p. 212.

[2] *Ibid.* chap. x. pp. 254, 256, 257.

[3] *Ibid.* chap. viii. p. 166.

T

pression derived from groups of building of such colossal dimensions must have been one of vast Imperial power and grandeur. The exterior of the thermæ was probably very plain, and even unsightly, and illustrates the Roman tendency to develop the interior of their buildings at the expense of the exterior, a tendency also to be noted in their basilicæ. Greek gymnasia, on the contrary, were ornamented on the exterior with colonnades and gateways. These great thermæ were, in fact, in every way characteristic of Rome. The baths at Pompeii and other provincial towns were merely establishments like the Oriental baths of Constantinople and Damascus at the present day ; but the extent of the Roman thermæ implies that thousands of the inhabitants of Rome spent a large portion of their time in the indolent recreations thus provided for them.

Agrippa and Alexander Severus were the principal founders of the public balneæ, as distinct from thermæ.

Adjecit ipse (Agrippa) aedilitatis suae commemoratione et ludos diebus undesexaginta factos et gratuita praebita balnea centum septuaginta quae nunc Romae ad infinitum auxere numerum.—Plin. *N. H.* xxxvi. 15, § 122.

Balnea omnibus regionibus addidit, quae forte non habebant, nam hodieque multa dicuntur Alexandri.—*Hist. Aug. Alex. Sev.* 39, 4.

The balneæ were used simply as baths, and had none

of the luxurious accessories attached to them which were found in the courts of the great thermæ, such as gymnasia, exedræ, and theatres. At Pompeii a tolerably perfect balneum is preserved, the principal room in which is a laconicum, or circular building with a domed roof, and the ground-plan of a similar establishment is to be found in the Capitoline map under the name Balneum Cæsaris.

There was hardly a town in the Empire which had not an amphitheatre large enough to contain vast multitudes of spectators.[1] The savage excitement of gladiatorial combats seems to have been almost a necessary of life to the Roman legionaries in their short intervals of inaction, and was the first recreation for which they provided in the places where they were stationed. At Rome a more effeminate mode of life was allowable, and even literary recreation might be tolerated in the halls of the thermæ; but when abroad, and in the subject provinces, the Roman was expected to wear the military dress, and to strike terror by a military ferocity of character.

It is very difficult to determine whence the Romans

---

[1] Sixty-two amphitheatres are enumerated by Clerisseau, *Antiquités de la France*, p. 92, as still existing in ruins. See also Friedländer, *Stttengesch. Roms.* ii. pp. 284, 404, where an exhaustive account is given of all the Roman amphitheatres.

took the elliptical shape of their amphitheatres. Gladiatorial combats were held from early times in the Forum,[1]

> D. Junius Brutus munus gladiatorium in honorem defuncti patris edidit primus.—Liv. *Epit.* xvi.
>
> Nam gladiatorium munus primum factum Romae in fero boario App. Claudio Q. Fulvio consulibus. Dederunt Marcus et Decimus filii Bruti Perae funebri memoria patris cineres honorando.—Val. Max. ii. 4, § 7,

and wild beasts hunted in the Circus; but until Curio built his celebrated double theatre of wood, which could be made into an amphitheatre by turning two semi-circular portions face to face,

> Theatra juxta duo fecit amplissima ligno (Curio, B.C. 50) cardinum singulorum versatili suspensa libramento; . . . . cornibus inter se coeuntibus faciebat amphitheatrum gladiatorumque praelia edebat.[2]— Plin. *N. H.* xxxvi. § 117,

we have no record of any special building in this peculiar form afterwards adopted. It may have been, therefore, that Curio's mechanical contrivance first suggested the elliptical shape. There is an elliptical

---

[1] B.C. 264.

[2] He made two large theatres of wood which could be turned so as to meet and form an amphitheatre, in which he gave gladiatorial combats. (Curio.)

amphitheatre at Sutrium in Etruria, excavated in the rock, which is by some antiquaries thought to be anterior to 'the time of Curio, and which might, in that case, have furnished the pattern of the Roman buildings.[1] Canina and Nibby, however, both pronounce it to be of Roman construction, and not earlier than the reign of Augustus.[2] It still remains, therefore, uncertain whence the Romans derived the elliptical form of their amphitheatres.[3]

As specimens of architecture, the amphitheatres are more remarkable for the mechanical skill and admirable adaptation to their purpose displayed in them, than for any beauty of shape or decoration. The hugest of all, the Coliseum, was ill proportioned and unpleasing in its lines when entire. The solid wall of its uppermost story gave it a heavy appearance; the width of the whole mass is too great in proportion to its height; and the columns and entablatures with which its exterior is decorated are structurally false, as they afford no real support to the building. But vast size and

---

[1] Dennis, *Etruria*, vol. i. p. 95.

[2] Nibby, *Analisi*, vol. iii. p. 142 ; *Giorn. Arcad.* xxiii. p. 311.

[3] Some of the later Greek stadia, as that of Aphrodisias in Caria, had two rounded ends, and may have suggested the form of the Roman amphitheatre.—Reber, *Gesch. der Baukunst*, p. 253.

massive dimensions force admiration even from the most critical, and produce an overwhelming impression of grandeur and immovable strength. Two architectural merits have been pointed out in the Coliseum—the impression of height and size conveyed by the tiers of arches rising one above another, and the graceful curves produced by the continuous lines of the entablatures as they cross the building.[1] But what the Roman emperor under whose auspices this great building was raised would doubtless have valued more than any elegances of design which could have been pointed out as perfect to him, is the adaptation of the structure to its purposes. After the great catastrophe at Fidenæ, where 50,000 persons were injured or killed by the breaking down of a wooden amphitheatre, solidity and safety were the principal requisites.

Quinquaginta hominum milia eo casu debilitata vel obtrita sunt. —Tac. *Ann.* iv. 63.

Supra viginti hominum milia gladiatorio numere amphitheatri ruina perierunt.—Suet. *Tib.* 40.

Free ingress and egress for crowds of spectators, as well as for any great personages who might attend, were also indispensable. A glance at the plan of the

---

[1] Fergusson, *Hist. of Arch.* vol. i. p. 304.

Coliseum will shew how admirably each of these objects was attained. The extraordinary solidity of the building removed all possibility of the failure of any part to bear whatever weight might be laid upon it, and the entrances,

JANUS QUADRIFRONS.

galleries, and vomitoria were, by the oval form of the building rendered so numerous that each seat in the whole cavea was accessible at once, and without difficulty. A system of carefully-arranged barriers in the passages effectually prevented confusion and excessive crowding.[1]

In endeavouring to adorn the great amphitheatre of the metropolis more richly than that of the provinces, its architect defeated his own object. Some of the provincial amphitheatres, as that of Capua, though in other respects like the Coliseum, shew a simpler, and therefore more natural exterior. When the Doric order is retained in all the tiers, it harmonises far better with the rude strength of such an edifice than the Corinthian and Ionic orders of the Coliseum.[2] At Verona and Pola a still further improvement is made by the rustication of the exterior.[3] At Nismes, on the other hand the faults of the Coliseum are aggravated by breaking the entablatures and introducing pediments over each front ; and in the small Amphitheatrum Castrense at Rome, where the Corinthian order is executed in brick,

---

[1] See *R. and C.* chap. ix. p. 237. It has been pointed out to me by a friend that some of the plans of Roman amphitheatres represent the passages leading from the exterior to the vomitoria with convergent sides, whereas in reality they were built with skew archways, so as to preserve the same width throughout. The plan of the Amphitheatre of Thysdrus in the *Monumenti dell' Inst.* 1852, vol. v. tav. 43, is correctly drawn in this respect.

[2] See Fergusson, *Hist. of Arch.* vol. i. p. 304.

[3] See Allason's *Pola*, and Maffei's *Verona*.

a lamentable illustration of Roman want of taste is exhibited.[1]

The naumachiæ at Rome were very similar to the excavated amphitheatres, of which many are still remaining,[2] but the central space was necessarily much larger, in order to make room for the combatant ships. The great Naumachia of Augustus was 1,800 feet long and 1,200 feet broad,[3] showing that the shape was oval, like that of an amphitheatre. But we know nothing of the extent or height of the spectators' seats. They were constructed of stone, for Suetonius tells us that the Naumachia of Domitian was pulled down at a subsequent time to furnish stone for the repairs of the Circus Maximus.

Naumachiam e cujus postea lapide maximus circus deustis utrimque lateribus extructus est.—Suet. Dom. 5.

The races and wild beast shows in the circi were among the most ancient and most favourite Roman amusements, and the buildings dedicated to these sports were numerous,

---

[1] See Le Grand, *Antiquities of Nismes;* Pelet, *L'Amphithéâtre de Nîmes;* and *R. and C.* chap. ix. p. 219.

[2] As at Sutri and Dorchester. See Stukely, *Iter Curiosum*, p. 166.

[3] See *Monum. Ancyr.* ed. Zumpt. At the sea-fights exhibited by Julius Cæsar there were 4,000 seamen and 1,000 marines engaged:

καὶ ναυμαχίαν ἐρετῶν τετρακισχιλίων ἐπιβεβηκότον ἐς μάχην χιλίων ἑκατέρωθεν —App. *B. C.* ii. 102.

and nearly equal in magnificence to the amphitheatres. The Circus Maximus, which was first provided with permanent seats for the spectators as early as the time of Tarquinius Priscus,

Foros in circo faciendos . . . . Tarquinius.—Liv. i. 56,

was successively restored and ornamented by the Republican Government in 325 and 174 B.C., and by Julius Cæsar, Augustus, Claudius, Domitian, and Trajan. The result was a building which, in dimensions and magnificence, rivalled the Coliseum, but has, unfortunately, proved far less durable, scarcely a vestige of it now being left. From the scattered notices which can be picked up here and there, and from the representations given upon the medals of Trajan, struck in honour of the circensian games of his reign, we gather the following information as to the architectural arrangements of the Circus Maximus in the time of the Empire, when it was entirely constructed of stone.[1] The exterior consisted of a triple range of arcades, one above the other, supported on piers, with the usual ornamental half-columns added. These tiers of arcades were of the same pattern as those of the Coliseum, only

---

[1] See Panvinius, *De Lud. Circ.* pp. 49, 50 ; Bianconi, *Descrizione dei Circi.*

on a much smaller scale.   The inner sides of the two lower arcades supported the seats, which were arranged as in an amphitheatre ; and the upper arcade formed a covered gallery, somewhat similar in appearance to the gallery which runs round the uppermost part of the Coliseum. Shops and offices of various kinds occupied the vaults of the lowest arcade.   At each end was a grand gateway, and at each corner of the rectangular end (or oppidum), and at the extremities of the hemicycle of the rounded end, were towers, called mœniana, where persons of distinction had places assigned to them.   The Emperor's pavilion, a projecting portico, was on the left of the carceres, and so placed that he could give the signal for starting from it.[1] The magnificence of the whole building after the restorations of Trajan was much celebrated.   Pliny especially notices the beauty of the long lateral arcades, which he says rivalled those of the great temples.   We can well understand that the effect of the whole was probably superior to that of any of the Roman amphitheatres or theatres.[2]

---

[1] Besides the Circus Maximus there were in Rome the Circus Flaminius and the Neronianus.   See *R. and C.* pp. 295, 313.

[2] A somewhat similar appearance to the exterior of the Circus is presented by the cryptoporticus of Diocletian's palace at Spalatro. See Adams's *Spalatro.*

Immensum latus circi templorum pulchritudinem provocat digna populo victore gentium sedes nec minus ipsa visenda, quam quae ex illa spectabantur.—Plin. *Panegyr.* 51.

The arcades gave a light and elegant appearance to the exterior, and the monotony of their long lines was broken by the gates and towers which rose above them. The interior was also agreeably diversified by the podium with its gilt railings, the tiers of stone seats, and the upper gallery, rising one above the other.[1]

The other circi of Rome were not equal in grandeur to the Circus Maximus. The Maxentian Circus, near the tomb of Cæcilia Metella, on the Appian road, the plan of which can still be easily traced, had no exterior colonnades, but a blank brick wall, pierced only here and there with doorways. There were only ten rows of seats, and the gallery above them was narrow and low.

The Theatre of Marcellus is the only Roman theatre of which the ruins are still left in Rome itself. Scarcely a vestige of the great theatres of Pompey and of Balbus can be found ; but Vitruvius has left so complete a description of the plan on which the Augustan theatres were built, that

---

[1] The Hippodrome at Constantinople, built by Constantine, shews the same architectural peculiarities. The lower story was built on piers with arches between them, and the upper decorated with columns. See Panvinius, *De Ludis Circ.*

we know pretty accurately what their architectural excellences and defects must have been. In speaking of amphitheatres, I have already anticipated much which applies equally to theatres. The exterior of the Theatre of Marcellus is similar to that of the Coliseum, but the details are worked out in a much purer style ; and though the same objection must be felt to the principle of exterior decoration with half-columns and entablatures, yet in the Theatre of Marcellus there was probably no solid wall, as in the Coliseum, forming the uppermost story, and the general appearance must therefore have been less heavy. The ground-plan of the Roman theatres differed from that of the Greek chiefly in the greater extent of the scena. This alteration was caused by the abolition of the chorus as intermediate between the spectators and actors, and the division of the place assigned to them, the orchestra, between the spectators and the stage proper. Thus the stage was brought much nearer to the spectators. The Greek cavea was a segment of a circle greater than a semicircle. The Romans, with their peculiar fondness for the semicircle above alluded to, reduced their cavea to that form— an alteration also required by the necessity of making more room for scenic displays, as the drama became less and less simple in its accessories, and depended more upon gorgeous effect than real dramatic art. Of the provincial Roman theatres, the best preserved is that of Aspendus, in Asia Minor, which shews not only the cavea, but the scena nearly entire. The theatre of Orange, in France, presents a complete scena, the outer wall of which is one of the grandest masses of Roman masonry extant, and free from the sham ornamental network of columns and entablatures so often found in such buildings.[1]

In domestic as well as in civil architecture, the Romans borrowed the most ornamental and luxurious parts of their houses, their peristylia, their triclinia, œci, exedræ, diætæ, sphæristeria, pinacothecæ, and bibliothecæ, from the Greeks. All these Greek names belong to the unessential and extraneous apartments attached, for the sake of recreation or pleasure, to the normal Roman house. In the primitive times of Rome, the houses of the citizens consisted of one principal central room, the atrium, round which the other parts of the house were grouped. In the atrium all domestic transactions took place ; the family hearth and the images of the Penates were there, meals were taken there, the mistress and her slaves worked there, the kitchen was there, the waxen masks of ancestors, the marriage-bed, and the money-chest of the paterfamilias stood there, visitors were

---

[1] At Vicenza there is a theatre called Teatro Olimpica, built by Palladio (1580), after the rules of Vitruvius, with the exception that it has an elliptical cavea.

received there, and it was in all respects the common room of the house. The name atrium is probably Etruscan:[1]

Atrium appellatum ab Atriatibus Tuscis illinc enim exemplum sumptum.—Varro, *L. L.* v. 161 ;

and the primitive atria were such as Vitruvius describes under the name "cavædium Tuscanicum," a large room, with a roof supported on four beams, two placed across from wall to wall, and two others at right angles to them, so as to leave a square opening in the centre, towards which the roof sloped down on all four sides from the walls. The opening in the centre was possibly, in the earliest times, intended only as a vent for the smoke ; but as the atrium became enlarged, it took the form of the impluvium. In the course of time, most of the domestic acts originally performed in the common hall were transferred to separate rooms, and the atrium came to be used only for the reception of guests, for the symbolical marriage-bed, for the images of ancestors, and for the lying in state of the dead. The extension of the atrium naturally caused the introduction of columns to support the roof, which had been unnecessary in the narrow, old-fashioned atria.[2]

---

[1] Müller, *Handbuch der Archæologie der Kunst*, S. 181.

[2] The enlargement of the house at Rome is contemporaneous with the enlargement of the Empire. One of these old atria is to be seen at Pompeii, No. 57, Strada Stabiana.

Multa in hac membra, atrium etiam ex more veterum.—Plin. *Ep.* v. 6, 15.

Cum invidendis postibus et novo sublime ritu moliar atrium.— Hor. *Od.* iii. 1, 46.

A further enlargement of the house then took place, and the atrium was left as the reception-room for clients and visitors, while another similar but larger court was built beyond it for the use of the family and intimate friends or guests. This was the cavædium. Both these courts are generally found in the houses at Pompeii, which were probably imitations of the ordinary houses of the metropolis, and not, as is sometimes supposed, planned on Greek models.[1] We find the Pompeian atria sometimes further enlarged by quadrangular recesses at the side furthest from the entrance, to which the term " alæ " used by Vitruvius probably applies. The space between the atrium and cavædium was filled up by a central square room, where it was customary to keep family records and documents ; this was called the tablinum : and on each side of it were passages (fauces) forming the communication between the atrium and cavædium.[2]

---

[1] The Pompeian houses all have the tablinum and fauces, which were essentially Italian parts of the house. They also correspond with the ground-plans of the houses given on the Pianta Capitolina.

[2] The position of the tablinum is almost entirely conjectural, and rests upon the arrangement of the Pompeian house. The name

The cavædium (Plin.), or cavum ædium (Vitruv. and
Varro), was a repetition of the atrium on a larger scale.
The most common methods of building it were those called
by Vitruvius Tetrastylon and Corinthium ; the former with
four pillars—one at each corner of the compluvium—and
the latter with rows of pillars supporting the timber of the
roof.[1] The central opening had a lacus or cistern to
receive the water from the roof, or a fountain and basin,
with flower-beds or shrubs and statuettes.

Nempe inter varias nutritur silva columnas.—Hor. *Ep.* i. 10, 22.
Nemus inter pulchra satum tecta.—Hor. *Od.* iii. 10, 5.

The intervals between the columns were sometimes closed
against cold winds, rain, or sun, by vela, or by boards which
could be removed like shutters.

Super atria velum
Candida purpureum simulatas inficit umbras.
                                        Ov. *Met.* x. 596.
Graves aulaea ruinas
In patinam fecere trahentia pulveris atri
Quantum non Aquilo Campanis excitat agris.
                                        Hor. *Sat.* ii. viii. 54.

---

tablinum is only mentioned by Vitruvius, Festus, Paul. Diac. and
Pliny, *Nat. Hist.* as a muniment room next the atrium.

[1] Besides these there were two other kinds of cavædia, the dis-
pluviatum with the roof sloped outwards, and the testudinatum
entirely covered with a lacunar.

U

Thus the atrium and cavædium, but especially the cavædium, were the central points towards which the other parts of the house converged ; and into them the cubicula and culina opened, and received light and air through the doorways. The chamber devoted to the Penates, after their removal from the atrium, was called the lararium, and was usually on the left of the atrium, near its entrance.

So far, the Roman houses were national in construction and arrangement. But as soon as it became fashionable at Rome to imitate Greek customs, and to borrow from the Greeks all the refinements and elegancies of life, the great houses at Rome were enlarged by the addition of various rooms and courts. The most common of these was the peristylium, which is found in many of the Pompeian houses, and was probably attached to the houses of all wealthy persons at Rome. This was a court surrounded with colonnades on three sides, or sometimes on all four sides, and containing a flower-garden (viridarium) in the centre. It differed from the cavædium only in having no dwelling rooms round it, and in having rows of columns as an indispensable part. If any further enlargements of a house were desired, they could be added to the peristylium. The most common of these extra rooms were the triclinia, several of which were sometimes built to suit the different seasons of the year. Besides triclinia, other extensions of the Roman houses, such as exedræ, which were semicircular projections or bays, furnished with seats for discussion or conversation; airy saloons called œci, opening upon gardens; basilicæ, or halls for business; pinacothecæ, and bibliothecæ, were all borrowed from the Greeks.

We have, unfortunately, not much to guide us in the endeavour to form an idea of the exterior appearance of the common houses in the streets of Rome. The interior arrangements of the Roman houses, and the domestic life of the Romans, have become known in minute detail to us from the Pompeian excavations, and may be most vividly realised by a walk through the streets of that resuscitated city, and a study of the contents of the Museum at Naples; but we are left to construct, from a few scanty notices, as we best may, the elevations and decorative peculiarities of their exteriors. The houses at Pompeii were mostly small and mean, and of the simplest plan. Scarcely any of them had upper floors, with the exception of those placed on sloping ground, where the first floor formed a kind of receding higher terrace. The fear of earthquakes, and the facility with which extensions could be made on the ground-floor, probably prevented the Pompeians from building lofty houses. But in Rome, where a large population was closely compressed round the great centres of business and pleasure,—the fora and the Imperial palaces,—it was necessary to raise the houses to a considerable height, to make the streets narrow, and to build projections into them. Even after the great Neronian conflagration, when parts at least of ten out of the fourteen regions were burnt down, the houses in Rome were probably far higher, and of a different construction from those of provincial towns, where no want of space was felt.

Pliny expressly mentions the lofty height of the houses as one of the characteristics of Rome in his time ; and the complaints of Juvenal as to their insecurity are well known :

> Tabulata tibi jam tertia fumant, tu nescis. —*Sat.* iii. 199.
>
> Quod spatium tectis sublimibus unde cerebrum
> Testa ferit.—*Sat.* iii. 269.
>
> Rarus venit in caenacula miles.—x. 18.

Nero fixed the extreme height to which houses might be raised. But though the houses were still very lofty, the general aspect of the streets must have been very different before and after the Neronian restoration. Cicero, comparing the old state of Rome with that of Capua, says that Rome was situated on uneven ground, and that the dwellings of the inhabitants were hoisted up and almost suspended in the air, that the streets were not of the best kind, while the alleys were execrably narrow, and that the metropolis could not bear comparison with her regularly built and wide-streeted neighbour Capua :

Romam caenaculis sublatam atque suspensam.—*De Leg. Agr.* ii. 96.

Omnis qui celsa scandit caenacula vulgus.—Prud. *c. Symm.* i. 580.

In Cicero's time the evil was probably at the worst : we hear of Rutilius Rufus urging this subject on the consideration of Government ; and Augustus abated it considerably by his wise regulations forbidding houses to be built more than seventy feet in height, and instituting a regular public service for enforcing this law, and taking supervision of the streets and buildings.[1]

Spatium urbis in regiones vicosque divisit instituitque ut illas annui magistratus sortito tuerentur.—Suet. *Aug.* 30.

Etiam libros totos et senatui recitavit et populo notos per edictum saepe fecit, scilicet Rutili de modo aedificiorum.—Suet. *Aug.* 89.

καίτοι καὶ ἐκείνων (τῶν ἀγορανόμων) καὶ τῶν δημάρχων τῶν τε στρατηγῶν πᾶσαν τὴν πόλιν, δεκατέσσαρα μέρη νεμηθεῖσαν, κλήρῳ προσταχθέντων (διένειμε.)—Dion. Cass. lv. 8.

κωλύσας (ὁ Σεβαστὸς Καῖσαρ) ἐξαίρειν ποδῶν ἑβδομήκοντα τὸ πρὸς ταῖς ὁδοῖς ταῖς δημοσίαις.—Strabo, v. 7.

---

[1] Aristides, the rhetorician, at a later date, the Antonine era, said that if the houses now piled one upon another in Rome were to be placed on level ground by the side of each other, they would reach to the Ionian Sea, covering the whole of Southern Italy.

Trajan restricted the height. of houses to sixty feet.

Statuens ne domorum altitudo sexaginta superaret pedes, ob ruinas faciles et sumtus siquando talia contingerent exitiosos.—Aur. Vict. *Epit.* xiii. 13.

The height of the houses in Rome must have had a considerable effect upon their exterior appearance, for it is plain that when the building was raised to a second or third story the rooms could no longer be lighted from the inner courts, but must have had windows looking out into the streets. Thus the tendency to make all the openings of the house turn inwards, which appears so plainly at Pompeii, must at Rome have been counteracted by the necessary conditions of their sites. But here attention must be drawn to the difference which prevailed in this respect between two great classes of private dwellings at Rome, the domus and the insula; for while the domus was in all probability seldom more than one or two stories in height, the insula, on the other hand, must have had five or six stories; and great inequalities in the appearance of the streets must have been the consequence. The small number of the domus in Rome in proportion to insulæ [1] shows that the former were the houses of men

---

[1] In the Catalogues of the Regionarii $\frac{\text{domus}}{\text{insulæ}} = \frac{1}{25}$. Preller, p. 86: Some houses were large. Petronius says of his house :

" Casa erat nunc templum est. Habet quattuor caenationes, cubicula

of wealth and importance—the palazzi of ancient Rome,
built according to the rules laid down by Vitruvius for
houses covering a large space of ground—while the latter,
inhabited by the middle and lower classes, and generally
built upon a narrow site, were carried up to the extreme
height allowed by law. Each insula contained a great
number of separate suites of rooms, or single rooms having
separate entrances, which were let as lodgings to families
or individuals.[1] These were called cœnacula.

An ordinance of the Twelve Tables fixed the space
which must be left clear between each insula or domus
at two feet and a half:

Ambitus circuitus ab eoque xii. tabularum interpretes ambitus
parietis circuitum esse describunt.—Varro, *L. L.* v. 22.

---

viginti, porticus marmoratas duas, xystum, cellationem, cubiculum in
quo ipse dormio, viperae hujus sessorium . . . . hospitium hospites
c capit."—Petron. *Sat.* 77.   "It was a cottage, but now it is as large
as a temple. There are four halls for entertainments, twenty rooms,
two marble porticoes, a large entry to sit in, a number of cellars,
my own bedroom, and this viper's drawing-room ; my spare rooms
will accommodate a hundred people." (*R. and C.* p. 412.)

[1] Rooms at the back or top of a domus were also sometimes used :

Posticulum hoc recepit, quum aedes vendidit.—Plaut. *Trin.* 194.

Caenaculum super aedes datum est, scalis ferentibus in publicum
obseratis aditu in aedes verso.—Liv. xxxix. 14.

Crassus owed his great wealth partly to successful speculation in
building a vast number of insulæ :

ὁρῶν τὰς συγγενεῖς καὶ συνοίκους τῆς Ῥώμης κῆρας ἐμπρησμοὺς καὶ

Ambitus proprie dicitur circuitus aedificiorum patens in latitudinem pedes duos et semissem.—Paull. *Diac. excerpt.* i. 5 ;

but this enactment appears to have been completely neglected before the time of Nero, for we find that in his restoration of the city it was expressly laid down, as a new regulation, that each building should have separate walls and a space (ambitus) left open all round it.

Erant tamen qui crederent, veterem illam formam salubritati magis conduxisse, quoniam angustiae itinerum et altitudo tectorum non perinde solis vapore perrumperentur.—Tac. *Ann.* xv. 43.

The insulæ must, as Preller remarks, have been very much like the large hotels of modern times, with one or more courts ; and they sometimes occupied the whole

---

συνιζήσεις διὰ βάρος καὶ πλῆθος οἰκοδομημάτων ἐωνεῖτο δούλους ἀρχιτέκτονας καὶ οἰκοδόμους.—Plut. *Crass.* ii.

Tabernae cum pergulis suis et caenacula equestria et domus locantur.—Orelli, *Inscr.* 4324.

Ex insulis fundisque tricies soldum
Ex pecore redeunt ter ducena Parmensi.

Mart. iv. 37.

Magno hospitium miserabile Romae.—Juv. iii. 166.

But without insurance offices the risks were great :

Si quid autem posset remedii fore ut ne tam adsidue domus Romae arderent.—Gell. xv. 1, 3.

block of buildings, bounded on all sides by streets, as in the case of the Louvre Hotel at Paris.[1] A passage of Vitruvius well explains the mode of construction usual in the insulæ: "The laws of the land do not allow any house wall built on public ground (*i.e.* towards the street) to be more than one and a half feet in thickness, and the other walls, in order to save space, are always built of the same thickness. But unburnt brick walls less than two or three bricks thick (a Roman brick being one foot in length) will not bear more than one story. The immense size and crowded population of Rome, however, make it necessary to have a vast number of habitations, and as the area is not sufficient to contain them all on the ground-floor, the nature of the case compels us to raise them in the air. And therefore lofty buildings supported on stone pillars, burnt brick-work, or ashlar, and furnished with numerous boarded floors, are made to supply the requisite number of separate apartments." [2]

After the great fire at Rome all the new houses were,

---

[1] The insulæ were then called vici from their resemblance to a vicus, *i.e.* a group of houses surrounded on all sides by streets. Insula also means a set of rooms in an insula.

[2] Vitruv. ii. 8, 17. One of the insulæ, in *Reg.* ix., named Felicles Insula, from the name of the owner, became proverbial for its

by Nero's orders, constructed partly of peperino stone
to resist fire, and had arcades built in front of all, from
the top of which help might be afforded in case of fire.[1]
The front ground-floor under the arcades would be probably occupied with shops. The interior of the insulæ
was very complicated, from the number of passages and
staircases required to reach all the separate lodgings, and
to arrange all the storehouses and offices of various kinds.
The building was under the charge of a dominus insulæ,
or insularius, an agent who accounted for the rents to
the proprietor.[2]

The passage of Vitruvius above quoted shows that
the insulæ were usually, in the time of Augustus, built
of unburnt brick in the lower parts, and of burnt bricks
or stone in the upper, with timbered floors. The Roman
unburnt bricks (lateres) were of two kinds, either whole
bricks one foot and a half in length and a foot wide,
or half bricks half a foot wide and one inch in thickness.[3]

---

enormous number of stories. Tertullian compares the Gnostic ideas
of different stages in heaven to this building:

Insulam Feliculae credas tanta tabulata coelorum.—Tertull. *Adv.
Val.* vii.

[1] These arcades were similar to those of Padua, Bologna, and
other Italian towns.

[2] See numerous names of insulæ in Preller, p. 92.

[3] See Vitruv. ii. 3.

In building a wall of the regulation thickness (a foot and a half), on one side a row of whole bricks was laid, and on the other a row of half bricks, and in the next layer a row of half bricks was laid upon the row of whole bricks, and a row of whole bricks upon the half bricks, so as to bind the wall together firmly by an interlacing structure.[1] Sometimes the bricks were laid in sloping rows diverging from a central line (herring-bone work, or opus spicatum, so called from its resemblance to the arrangement of the seeds in an ear of corn), and confined by stone edgings. These unburnt brick walls were always covered with stucco (tectorium or albarium) made with great care, sometimes of pounded marble chips, and were generally painted in bright colours, as may be seen in the streets of Pompeii. When concrete (fartura) was used for the core of the wall, it was some-times cased with stones placed irregularly (opus incertum),[2] and was then always covered with stucco ; or it was cased with small diamond-shaped stones arranged in a regular chess-board fashion (opus reticulatum), in which case

---

[1] Winckelmann, *Arch. des Anciens*, œuvres, vol. ii. p. 545. Roman bricks were sometimes of a much larger size. Those used in vaulting were generally wedge-shaped.

[2] It is doubtful whether the term " opus incertum " includes ashlar-work.

stucco was not always used. Walls of unburnt brick
were also sometimes cased with opus reticulatum, and
occasionally brick and concrete were mixed in alternate
layers and cased with stucco or opus reticulatum or
incertum. The larger houses and public buildings were
built with solid walls of squared stones, reaching completely across the whole breadth of the wall, and laid
in equally-sized courses (opus isodomum), or in unequally-
sized courses (opus pseudisodomum).

The principal entrance of a domus stood a little back
from the line of the street in a recess (vestibulum), the two
projecting sides of which were frequently occupied by
shops opening into the street.[1] These vestibules were of
various depths. At Pompeii they are generally very small,
but in some of the large houses at Rome the vestibule
was ornamented with trophies which would require a
considerable space.

An tu illa in vestibulo rostra an spolia quum adspexisti domum
tuam te introire putas?—Cic. *Phil.* ii. 28.

Barbario postes auro spoliisque superbi
Procubuere.—*Æn.* ii. 504.
Quin etiam veterum effigies ex ordine avorum
Antiqua e cedro . . . . vestibulo adstabant.

Æn. vii. 177.

---

[1] Becker derives vestibulum from *ve*, apart, and *stabulum*, a place
to stand in apart from the house ; as *prostibulum*, *vecors*, *vesanus*.

Hujus enim stat currus aeneus alti
Quadrijuges in vestibulis.—Juv. *Sat*. vii. 125.

They were occasionally ornamented with pilasters or a portico of Greek construction. In the case of Nero's Golden House the vestibule must have been a splendid court surrounded with arcades and ornamented by the huge colossal statue of the emperor.[1] The threshold and lintel (limen inferius and superius) and the doorposts (antepagmenta) were of wood or stone, according to the wealth of the owner. There were frequently inscriptions or signs over the door, marking the house as in mediæval times,[2]

Domitianus natus est . . . . regione urbis sexta ad malum Punicum —Suet. *Dom*. 1.
Natus est Augustus . . . . ad Capita bubula regione Palati.—Suet. *Oct*. 5.

and sometimes a parrot taught to say "Salve" or "Χαῖρε" was hung up in a cage.

Pica salutatrix si tibi, Lause, placet.—Mart. vii. 87.
Pica loquax certa dominum te voce saluto
Si me non videas esse negabis avem.
Mart. xiv. 76.
Quis expedivit psittaco suum χαῖρε.—Pers. *Prol*. 8.
Super limen cavea pendebat aurea, in qua pica varia intrantes salutabat.—Petron. 28.

---

[1] See *R. and C.* p. 165.   [2] As the orange, the ox heads.

Door bells do not seem to have been usual, though bells were sometimes employed for giving signals of other kinds; but there were always knockers of metal to the doors, at which every one except inmates of the house were expected to knock.[1]

Occlusa janua est interdius? Pultabo.—Plaut. *Most.* ii. 2. 14.
Ubi estis? servi. Occludite aedis, ubi hanc ego tetulero intra limen.
—Plaut. *Cist.* iii. 18.
Quid miser expavescis? ad clamorem servi, ad tinnitum aeris, aut januae impulsum?—Sen. *De Ira,* iii. 35.

As carriages were not used commonly in the streets before the third century,[2] few of the principal house entrances were large enough to admit them, but they

---

[1] The doors at Rome generally opened inwards, contrary to the Greek fashion, as shown in the comedies taken from the Greek. It was the custom in Greece to knock before going *out* in order that any one passing might avoid being struck by the door opening outwards. But in later times many doors at Rome also opened outwards:

Ταύτης τῆς οἰκίας αἱ κλισιάδες θύραι μόναι τῶν ἐν τῇ Ρώμῃ δημοσίων τε καὶ ἰδιωτικῶν οἴκων εἰς τὸ ἔξω μέρος ἀνοίγονται.—Dionys. *Hal. Ant. Rom.* v.
Sed foris concrepuit nostra: quinam exit foras?—Plaut. *Bacch.* ii. 2, 56.
Lucius Titius aperto pariete domus suae quatenus stillicidii rigor et lignorum projectus competebat januam in publico aperuit.—*Digest.* viii. 2, 41.

[2] See Friedländer, *Sittengesch. Roms,* S. 52.

were of course wide enough to admit the sedans of considerable size in which Romans often went out into the town. There were generally side and back doors of smaller size, without vestibules, leading into the side streets.

The ground-floors both of the domus and insulæ were, as has been stated, usually occupied by shops, and therefore rooms on the ground-floor had doors opening on the inner courtyard and had no windows. In the lofty courts of the insulæ, where the ground-floor rooms would naturally be very dark, they were probably used as storerooms and offices. The rooms on the upper floors opened by windows on the street, which were often provided with balconies or projections supported on brackets and called mœniana, pergulæ, or podia.

καὶ εἴ τινες ἦσαν ξύλων ἐξοχαί (πολλαὶ δὲ αὗται κατὰ τὴν πόλιν) πῦρ προσετίθεσαν.—Herodian, vii. 12, 5.

These balconies must have improved the exterior appearance of the houses very much by breaking the flat surface of the wall. From them shows in the streets were surveyed and speeches sometimes delivered.

Ex superiore parte aedium per fenestras in Novam viam versas (habitabat enim rex ad Jovis Statoris) populum Tanaquil alloquitur. —Liv. i. 41.

Comicae autem (scenae) aedificiorum privatorum et maenianorum

habent speciem prospectusque fenestris dispositos imitatione com-
munium aedificiorum rationibus.—Vitruv. v. 6(8).

Pars ex tectis fenestrisque prospectant (at Syracuse).—Liv. xxiv. 21.

Quotiens rimosa et curta fenestris
Vasa cadant quanto percussum pondere signent
Et laedant silicem.—Juv. iii. 270.

Per quam demisso quoties tibi fune pependi
Alterna veniens in tua colla manu.

Propert. v. (iv.) 7, 17.

Et quantum licuit consurgere tectis
Una replet turbae facies, undare videres
Ima viris, altas effulgere matribus aedes.

Claudian, *De Sex. Cons. Honor. Panegr.* 544.

Martial gives a lively picture of the spectators on the line of the Emperor Trajan's entry into Rome:

Quando erit ille dies quo campus et arbor et omnis
Lucebit Latia culta fenestra nuru.—Mart. x. 6.

The windows were closed with lattice-work or plates of talc, or sometimes with glass, to keep out the cold and wind, and had folding shutters.[1]

---

[1] The subject of glass windows in ancient houses is fully discussed in Hirt, *Gesch. der Bauk.* iii. 1, Beilage C. He thinks that the expression "specularia" denotes glass windows and = specularia vitra. The word which is used in Philo, *Leg. ad Caium*, § 45, probably means glass; in which case the palace of Caligula had glass windows. In the public baths at Pompeii a bronze casement with panes of glass was found. Mazois, *Pal. de Scaur.* vii. p. 97.

προστάττει τας ἐν κύκλῳ θυρίδας ἀναληφθῆναι τοῖς ὑάλῳ λεύκη διαφανέσι

The roofs of the houses in Rome were sometimes gabled (pectenata) exactly like modern houses, and it is a mistake to suppose that only temples had gables, and that the streets of Rome showed a succession of flat roofs. Some of the pictures of houses in the Pompeian house decorations show gabled roofs, and Cicero, writing to his brother, speaks of the roof of a house as having more than one gable.

Pectenatum tectum dicitur similitudine pectinis in duas partes divisum, ut testudinatum in quattuor.—Paull. Diac. p. 213. Mueller.

Absolutum offendi in aedibus tuis tectum : quod supra conclavia non placuerat tibi esse multorum fastigiorum, id nunc honeste vergit in tectum inferioris porticus.—Cic. *Ad Quint. fratr.* iii. 1, 14.

> Quid nunc ingentia mirer
> Aut quid partitis distantia tecta trichoris.
>
> Stat. *Silv.* i. 3, 57.

Simulacrum ejus in trichoro consistit, positum ex Thebaico marmore.—*Hist. Aug. Pesc. Nig.* 12.

παραπλησίως λίθοις οἳ τὸ μὲν φῶς οὐκ ἐμποδίζουσιν, ἄνεμον δὲ εἴργουσιν καὶ τὸν ὑφ' ἡλίου φλογμόν.—Philo, *Leg. ad Caium.* § 45.

Glebas nitri e nave subsidisse quibus accessis permixta harena litoris translucentis novi liquoris fluxisse rivos et hanc fuisse originem vitri.—Plin. *N. H.* xxxvi. 65.

Porticus specularibus muniuntur.—Plin. *Ep.* ii. 17, 4.

Quod non in caldarium suum latis specularibus diem admiserat.—Senec. *Ep.* 86, 11.

> Hibernis objecta Notis specularia puros
> Admittunt soles et sine faece diem.—Mart. viii. 14.

The regular triangular pediment, however, was peculiar to the temples of the gods, the palaces of the Cæsars, and some of the other public buildings. The eaves sometimes projected considerably over the street, and enactments were passed limiting their size.

Ne quis in suggranda protectove supra eum locum quo vulgo iter fiet inve quo consistetur id positum habeat cujus casus nocere cui possit.—*Digest.* ix. 3, 5.

Et superne subgrundas proclinatas supra, quae tabulis et coriis firmiter fixis continentur.—Vitruv. x. xv. (xxi.) 1

Domed roofs and quadrilateral roofs were sometimes built, but naturally these were for the most part confined to small angular or circular edifices, such as the Temple of the Penates in the Forum, or the so-called Temple of Vesta on the river bank. The "cavædium testudinatum" of Vitruvius was roofed in this way.

Tectum inter et laquearia tres senatores haud minus turpi latebra quam detestanda fraude sese abstrudunt.—Tac. *Ann.* iv. 69.

Flat roofs were the most frequent in the Roman domus, the other kinds being more adapted to the insulæ. Upon the top of their flat roofs gardens were constructed, and filled with flowers and fruit-trees, and seats were made for basking in the winter sun. The usual outer covering of the roofs when flat was of stone, stucco, or metal. For sloping roofs, thatch or shingles, tiles, slates, or metal plates were used. Pliny states that, until the time of the war with Pyrrhus, all Rome was roofed with shingles.

Scandala contectam fuisse Romam Pyrri usque ad bellum annis cccclxx. Cornelius Nepos auctor est.—Plin. *N. H.* xvi. 15.

The common form of dwelling-house in those times was probably the primitive hut (tugurium), or at best the old Tuscan form of the atrium, a small court with a square impluvium supported by four beams. The Roman tiles were of two kinds, flat tiles and smaller curved tiles. The flat tiles had raised rims at the sides, except at the upper end, which was pushed under the tile next above on the roof. The small curved tiles were then laid over the joined edges of the lower ones, and formed a complete protection for the joints.[1]

Quod meas confregisti imbrices et tegulas ibi dum condignam te sectatus simiam.—Plaut. *Mil. Glor.* ii. 6, 24.

Tempestas venit, confringit tegulas imbricesque.—Plaut. *Most.* i. 2, 25.

To say that the dwelling-houses of Rome presented in general an irregular appearance is no doubt correct;[1] but when their architectural pretensions are condemned

---

[1] Cf. Rein in Becker's *Gallus,* ii. p. 271.

as inferior to those of modern houses, it may be questioned whether such an opinion has not been too much influenced by the aspect of the Pompeian houses. It has been shown that contrasts were drawn by Roman writers between the metropolis and the provincial towns, especially with reference to the size and height of the houses ; and in the crowded parts of Rome, and along the principal thoroughfares leading to the great roads, as the Via Lata and the Alta Semita, which seem to correspond to the modern Corso and Via della Porta Pia, nearly all the dwelling-houses were probably lofty, well built, and furnished in the upper stories with handsome windows and balconies, and with porticoes or arcades projecting over shops on the ground-floor.

At the same time, on account of the hilly nature of the site and the interruption of the lines of the streets by the great fora and public buildings, but few long wide streets could have existed in ancient Rome. There was apparently a constant necessity for edicts providing against the excessive crowding and blocking up of the streets by vehicles. Carriages or carts, with few exceptions, were not allowed to pass during the first ten hours of the day, and a clearance of the projecting mœniana and the stalls of all tradesmen and hucksters had to be made periodically.

Mœniana sustulit omnia, fabricari Rbmae priscis quoque vetita legibus. A.D. 368.—Amm. Marc. xxvii. 9, 10.

Martial complains bitterly of the noises at night, from the traffic in the streets, which would not allow him to sleep, and praises Domitian for having cleared the barbers', cooks', butchers', and winesellers', stalls away, and made it at length possible to pass freely along the streets.

> Tonsor caupo coquus lanius sua limina servant.
> Nunc Roma est, nuper magna taberna fuit.—vii. 61, 9.

Nos transeuntis risus excitat turbae, et ad cubile est Roma taedio fessis, dormire quoties libuit, imus ad villam.—xii. 57, 26.

It has been remarked that, with all the Roman passion for Greek forms of architecture, yet the names of the architects employed at Rome which have come down to us are mainly Roman,[1] and that even before the time when the first Greek architect, Hermodorus of Salamis, is mentioned as employed at Rome, we find a Roman, Cossutius, engaged in the erection of the great Temple of Zeus Olympius at Athens in the reign of Antiochus Epiphanes:

---

[1] Hirt, *Gesch. der Baukunst*, ii. p. 257 ; Ampère, *Hist. Rom. à Rome*, vol. iv. p. 77.

Antiochus rex cum esset pollicitus, magna sollertia scientiaque summa civis Romanus Cossentius nobiliter est architectatus.—Vitruv. vii. Praef. 15.

The architect of the famous Temple of Honour and Virtue, dedicated by Marius, was a Roman, C. Mutius; and Cicero employed a Roman architect in the erection of the chapel in memory of his daughter Tullia. Vitruvius praises three books on architecture written by the Romans Fufitius, Varro, and Publius Septimius.[1] Under Augustus, besides Vitruvius himself, who was an Italian by birth but a Greek by education, we find only Valerius of Ostia mentioned as employed in architectural works, and a freedman, L. Cocceius. Again in Nero's time, the great architects Severus and Celer have Roman names; and Rabirius, the architect of Domitian, appears to have been a Roman. A Greek artist, Apollodorus, first comes into prominent notice in the reigns of Trajan and Hadrian, but it is probable that a Roman, Frontinus, was also largely patronised by these emperors.

But in the Imperial times a perfect army of architects and builders must have been kept up in order to execute new works or keep the old buildings in repair. It is said that 700 architects were employed by Nero and

---

[1] Three architects mentioned by Cicero, Cyrus, Chrysippus, and Corumbus, have Greek names, but were possibly slaves.

Trajan for the sole purpose of attending to the supply of water for the city. The whole number engaged in different parts of the world under these emperors must therefore have numbered many thousands. We find the governor of Nicomedia asking for an architect from Rome to construct a serviceable aqueduct for the city, as two previous attempts, possibly by local architects, had not succeeded. Hadrian, it is well known, was his own architect in many cases, and prided himself upon having designed the great Temple of Venus and Rome ; but he also employed vast numbers of architects to assist in his minor works.

(Hadrian) Namque ad specimen legionum militarium fabros, per-pendiculatores, architectos, genusque cunctum extruendorum maenium seu decorandorum in cohortes centuriaverat.—Aur. Vict. *Epit.* 14.

Several names of ancient architects have been found at Terracina, Pozzuoli, in Spain, and at Bonn, all of which are Roman ; and the probable reasons for the employment of Romans in preference to Greek are not difficult to assign.[1] The Roman emperors sought, above all things, durability and colossal size in their architectural works While therefore Greek sculptors would doubtless be pre-ferred for the decorative parts of the building, the designing

[1] Ampère, *Hist.* p. 79.

of the whole on a large scale, and the strength of the construction, would be best entrusted to a Roman, who might well be more an engineer than an architect. In the raising of huge stones, and the construction of enormous arches, the Romans had more practical talent and skill than the Greeks ; and as these were principal matters in their huge buildings, it does not seem strange that Roman architects were more frequently employed than Greek. The profession of an architect at Rome was considered inferior to that of a military engineer, a natural result of the supremacy of the military and political elements in the Roman national character.

The architect about whom we know most, Vitruvius, was really a military engineer, and had served in that capacity during a great part of his life. He would have so remained, or at least would not have published his scientific views on architecture, had he not seen that Augustus was something more than a mere hard, practical statesman, and possessed great refinement of taste, and a desire to introduce into Rome a love for the beautiful in art.

Ad exitum vitae . . . . haec tibi scribere cepi . . . . quod attenderem te non solum de vita communi curam habere, sed etiam de opportunitate publicorum aedificiorum ut majestas imperii publicorum aedificiorum egregias haberet auctoritates.—Vitruv. i. praef.

Vitruvius's chief object was to perpetuate the great principle

of purity and simplicity in design and elegance in proportion laid down by the chief Greek architects, and to
counteract the vulgar taste for coarse and overladen
decoration, which he saw prevailing at Rome. While we
sympathise with Vitruvius in his dislike of the Roman
fondness for accumulation of unmeaning ornament, and
with his protests against their neglect of constructive truth,
we cannot help regretting that he failed to see wherein
the real strength of Roman architecture consisted, and in
what direction its true development lay, and that he
encouraged instead that slavish imitation of the Greeks,
which was as fatal to the growth of genuine Roman
architecture as it was to the development of a really
national Roman literature. The horizontal lines of Greek
architecture, and the necessarily narrow areas of their
buildings, were never brought into living union with the
peculiarly Roman method of construction by the arch.
We can derive much pleasure, it is true, from the Romano-
Greek buildings ; yet we feel that they are not a real
embodiment of Roman ideas, but a composite mass of
heterogeneous elements, which no skill can reduce success-
fully into a harmonious whole.

The same mixed character belongs to their literature,
in which their real natural characteristics, their deep and
practical views of human nature, their political and military

genius, are everywhere overlaid and dressed up with Grecian art, and forced into Grecian forms. A native Roman style of architecture was never developed by the Romans themselves, but in their arched structures they left to succeeding ages the rudiments of the grandest and most perfectly expressive of all styles of architecture, the Gothic. So in the same way the intense interest in human life, and the moral and practical spirit which pervaded their literature, and formed its support, has, like the hidden arches of their buildings, proved the framework upon which some of the noblest creations of modern intellect have been reared.

The Romans were the greatest builders that the world has ever seen; but they never succeeded in developing any system of decorative architecture. They were an arch-building yet not an architectural nation. They planted in the West and the East, in the remotest part of Britain and the deserts of Petra and Palmyra, imperishable monuments of their engineering and masonic skill; but in all their attempts to create ornamental structures they failed to produce anything more than gigantic or grotesque imitations of Greek art. From an æsthetical point of view, therefore, the study of their buildings is barren. They did not possess an eye for fine proportion of outline, or symmetrical and harmonious combination of details. A certain vulgar love of gorgeous and costly ornament, and an incapacity for appreciating the beauty of simplicity and purity, pervade all their most elaborate buildings. But as historical monuments, illustrative of the peculiar genius and character of the Romans, the study of Roman structures is most important and valuable. We see embodied in them that indomitable energy and strength of purpose which bridged the valleys and tunnelled through the hills ; that conviction of the grandeur of their empire and destiny which could not be satisfied with anything short of the colossal and imperishable ; that strong practical utilitarianism which constantly sought means to improve the conditions of human life, and render the earth a more convenient habitation for men, and at the same time that intense passion for fierce excitement and luxurious enjoyment, which made them lavish untold wealth in the construction of stupendous amphitheatres and thermæ.

THE END.